P. B. de Cartwright.

March 52.

KOREAN REPORTER

To Elizabeth

Villagers moving South   (*Planet News*)

KOREAN
REPORTER

by
René Cutforth

LONDON
ALLAN WINGATE
12 Beauchamp Place SW3

Printed and made in Great Britain
by William Clowes & Sons Ltd.
London & Beccles

for

ALLAN WINGATE (PUBLISHERS) LTD.
12 Beauchamp Place, London, S.W.3

First published 1952

PREFACE

I WAS the B.B.C.'s special correspondent in Korea from the beginning of December 1950 until the end of July 1951, so that I arrived in time for the winter retreat from the Yalu River, saw the advance across the 38th Parallel in the spring, and the beginning of the Peace Talks at Kaesong in the summer —a slice of history which will keep the military and political experts in earnest debate for years.

This book has no contribution to make to that debate, but it tries to answer one question—the first question asked by friends of any returned traveller.

"Haven't seen you for some time," the friends say.

"No, I've been away."

"Really. Where to?"

"I've been in Korea."

"No, really? WHAT WAS IT LIKE?"

There are only two answers to this, one is:

"Well——"

The other is to write a book about it.

R. C.

LIST OF ILLUSTRATIONS

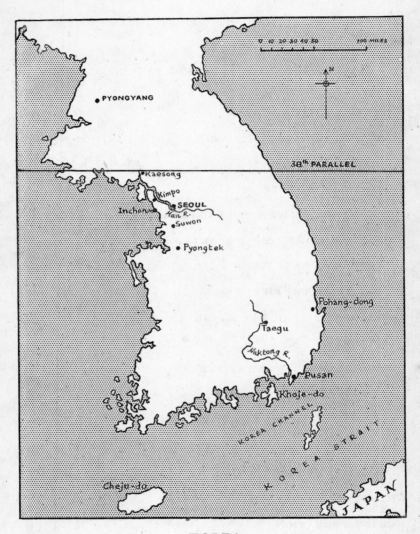

KOREA

CHAPTER I

THE plane bumped to a stop. We were in Korea. I undid the
safety strap and rose slowly and painfully to my feet, groping
about in the brownish light among my belongings. All my
movements were heavy and clumsy, partly because I was wearing about thirty pounds of clothing, and partly because I was
numb with cold. Hands, feet and ankles all refused their
function, calves were very stiff, lips could make only a sort of
botched approximation to speech. I dropped my kitbag over
the sill of the plane's door and fell down the metal ladder with
my typewriter and recorder. It was like slipping over the side
into a cold swimming bath, and I drew in my breath and looked
about quickly for shelter. There was none. It was one o'clock
in the morning in early December and a pitch black night. A
wind which I was to get to know well moaned gently across the
Taegu airstrip and carried away behind me the last shreds of my
morale. I was actually beginning to whimper with discomfort
when Cyril Page, my television colleague, a comparatively old
hand in Korea—he'd been there three months—came across to
me and began to whisper urgently. "All these fellows," said
Page, indicating our late fellow travellers, "are saying 'What
about staying here for tonight and going to Kimpo tomorrow?'
and finally they'll all stay. Now look, it'll be just as cold and
bloody in the plane tomorrow, and anyway it's only an hour
and a half more to Kimpo. We can't get much colder than we
are. Let's get it over, what do you say?" "Right," I said, "but
let's get out of this wind."

"There's sure to be a plane going on," said Page and disappeared into the darkness.

A few moments later he was back. "Get your luggage," he
said, "quick." We sprinted about a hundred yards into the
darkness and I almost ran into the plane he had discovered, a

vague shape squatting on the runway, black against the navy blue sky.

"Here we are," said Page. "Here's the ladder, don't strike matches, get in and sit where you like. The great thing is to be in first. Then they can't throw us off. It's going to Kimpo. The mechanic told me." In brief careful flashes of his electric torch, illuminating a few feet around us, we stacked our luggage in the tail and seated ourselves on pierced metal seats along the walls of the interior, and waited. We were out of the wind at any rate. "Don't smoke," warned Page. "It gives them an excuse to throw you off."

As I sat there, groping in my kitbag for a bottle of whisky, I had a sudden intense pang of nostalgia for the bright lights, soft chairs and wonderful American drinks in the Tokyo Press Club we had left only four hours before. How fantastic, there, had these clothes seemed when I first put them on under the expert eye of Page.

"Go on, put it on, you'll need it."

"But, hell, I've got two shirts on already."

"You'll need three. Put it on. I tell you it's cold over there. How many pairs of long pants have you got?"

"One."

"You need at least two, probably three."

At last I was dressed. I had on two vests, three shirts, two pullovers, two pairs of long pants. A battledress, plus windproof trousers. And over all that a parka—a wonderful hooded, belted American coat, lined with silk pile like short fur. Its inside flaps fastened with a zipper and then buttoned over that like a double breasted coat. You could pull the hood tight against your face with a string. I had my trousers clipped into three pairs of socks—one of them ski-ing socks, and calf-length boots with thick felt inner soles.

I had staggered about the Press Club bedroom like a diver, laughing. Fantastic garments!

The only fantastic thing about them now, I thought gloomily, warming the neck of the whisky bottle in my gloves so that it wouldn't hurt my mouth, is their signal failure to keep the cold out.

Just as I was taking a swallow of the fiercely cold whisky, a light snapped on, and I was caught with the guilty bottle to my mouth. It was strictly forbidden to carry alcoholic drink in service planes. The American air force sergeant who stood there looking at us had not apparently heard of this rule.

"If you've got a spare drop . . . ?" he said, and I handed over the bottle. He looked terribly tired.

"You goin' to Kimpo?"

"Hope so."

"Won't be long now. Due out in ten minutes. What's your weight, brother?"

"Two-hundred pounds in these clothes," I said.

"And your baggage?"

"About eighty pounds."

"Yeah, we can do that I think, but we're a bit full. Have to see what the pilot says."

Footsteps sounded outside as the passengers began to arrive. They swung themselves clumsily up the short ladder, headed by an American lieutenant-colonel with a good broad courageous face. He was followed by three G.I.s, two of them drunk, and an American air force lieutenant.

The soupy brown light from the only bulb inside the plane was sufficient to give a bald summary of its appearance. It was an olive-green metal tube we were sitting in, about seven feet across, and about two-thirds of its length was occupied by a great humped shape six feet high, covered with canvas and roped to the floor. Protruding pieces suggested a pile of machine guns. In the remaining third, the tail, were the passengers and their luggage. The colonel, the lieutenant, Page and I sat on that part of the metal wall seat which the machine guns were not using. The others sat on their luggage on the floor.

There was a big bucket behind a curtain at the extreme tail end of the plane, for use as a latrine. The air force sergeant was busy tightening the ropes which held down the pile of machine guns.

"It's a hell of a load," he said conversationally, standing back to admire his handiwork. "Fortunately, I'm not flying with you."

3

When the pilot came up the ladder, he stood in the middle of us with his hands on his hips, looking at the canvas-covered pile. He was a tall, fair young man and even in that light you could see his eyes were red-rimmed with desperate fatigue.

"I'm not taking that," he said, "it's just about double my load by the look of it, and for Chrissakes, four, five, six, seven passengers."

"Major Heidegger wanted to talk to you about it, sir."

"I'll be very interested to hear what he has to say."

The pilot leaped to the ground and was immediately hailed by a fruity voice outside the plane. Snatches of the shouted conversation mangled by the wind drifted up into the plane.

"I know goddam well how well they've been weighed," shouted the pilot. "The goddam weighing clerk holds one up in his hands and says, 'About twenty pounds. Right, load on fifty of these,' he says, 'and that'll be a thousand pounds.' And every goddam one of them weighs twenty-seven pounds."

The argument lasted about five minutes; then the pilot climbed aboard again. "O.K.," he sang back over his shoulder at the major, as one who has the unanswerable last word, "O.K. Let's hope we get there."

The sergeant jumped off. The door was closed. The engine roared. The brown light brightened from Van Dyck to mulligatawny and we were off. The colonel took out of his parka pocket a paper-backed book called "The Terror of Bar 71," on whose cover a pair of gigantic men wrestled for a six-shooter, and began to read.

From the very first that trip did not go well. The flight engineer talking to me afterwards said: "Well I reckon we made all of three-hundred feet in the first twelve miles." I didn't know then, but I know now that all air strips in Korea, except the coastal ones, are the bottoms of bowls with high rims of peaks, usually two or three thousand feet high. If you don't very soon get above them, then you have to double and zig-zag about between them, and this is very much easier in daylight than at night.

About ten minutes after we took off we began to make very sharp and uncomfortable turns. The luggage shifted and rolled

4

on the floor and something fell down 'slap' at the tail end of the plane and brought all our heads round abruptly. At this point a small, dark man came precipitately out from the front of the machine and yelled: "For Chrissakes get yourselves and your baggage out of the tail and up front a bit." This order was obeyed almost before he'd finished speaking. We piled ourselves and our baggage into the small space between the seats and the machine guns and the walls. One of the drunk G.I.s had to be treated as baggage. He was flung violently across a couple of kitbags, where he lay retching miserably.

"The pilot don't want any of you to go to the can. We don't want no weight in the tail."

The door to the front closed behind him and I found myself looking—staring—at the air force lieutenant who was the only one amongst us who knew what was happening. Then I saw that everybody else too, except the colonel and the retching G.I., was looking at him. And as I watched, the colonel put down "Bar 71" on his knee, took off his steel spectacles and stared intently across at the lieutenant himself.

The lieutenant was sucking at an empty pipe. He was well aware that he was under scrutiny, and his face was quite empty of expression. I noticed that he made his every small movement very slow and deliberate. Suddenly, the plane gave a frightful lurch which flung me on to the floor. The engine abruptly changed its note for a higher, louder one. The sober G.I.—he was a small bald man—suddenly went green and shut his eyes. We were staring at the lieutenant as criminals awaiting sentence stare at the judge, and now he could no longer appear to disregard us. He took the empty pipe very deliberately out of his mouth, gave us a slow reassuring smile and said: "I'm well acquainted with the guy up front and he's a very good pilot." He then corked his mouth up with the pipe again and sat back listening.

We waited for the next manifestation. It came about four minutes later. The plane made a long, terrifying, scooping movement sideways through the air, like the swoop and check of a paper dart, but sideways, and almost simultaneously the small dark man came out from the forward doorway and chanted:

5

"Get your parachutes on." He added redundantly: "We're having a little trouble up front and you may have to jump."

I admired the way the small dark man whistled as his nimble fingers flew about the fastenings of the parachutes. The lieutenant helped too, slowly, with his reassuring smile, looking into our eyes as he talked. The dark man said: "I'm opening the door now, but I want nobody to jump until he's told. When you go out, go headfirst, fold your arms this way, count one thousand, two thousand, three thousand . . ." he went on and on. The plane bucked and struggled paper-dart-wise. As the dark man opened the door, we were suddenly drowning in a tempest of freezing air.

The lieutenant and the dark man had a small conference and then the dark man went forward again and the lieutenant shouted to us above the noise. "Just a minute. The situation is that we're having trouble with the de-icer. We're losing height and we haven't a hell of a lot more height to lose. If you jump now, your parachute won't open, but we'll come to one of these deep valleys in a minute and then it'll be safe to let go. The two civilians, the correspondents, will go first."

He smiled around at us. He was a wonderful chap. Very nearly he persuaded me that it was all in the day's work. Not quite though. I was so frightened I felt myself to be suffering from a kind of paralysis. My mind was going so fast that all action seemed to me to be in slow motion. The lieutenant's speech had seemed to me to last about twenty minutes. I had lived half a dozen lives while they were buckling my parachute. It seemed about half a lifetime more before I realised that the plane wasn't jolting any more and seemed to be riding evenly. The engines still kept up their higher pitch screaming.

The dark man came back. "We're over a deep valley now," he said, "but the pilot thinks he has a chance to make Kimpo. So he's not ordering you to jump. If anybody fancies he's better off jumping, he'd better go now."

There were no takers. Except for the lieutenant, we all slumped where we stood. The dark man shut the door. He spoke for a minute or two to the lieutenant and then disappeared forward again, scrambling past the machine guns.

6

The colonel looked at each of us very intently in the face for about ten seconds. Then he said:"I never did like airplanes." The lieutenant sat down and said conversationally, "Well, you see, the initial trouble was the big load. They couldn't make enough height to take the normal route, so we had to go wandering about among the peaks. So the navigator only knew in a general sort of way where we were. And then the de-icer gave up and we were losing height and the pilot thought he might smash up on the big ridge. But now he reckons he crossed the big ridge five minutes ago, with about thirty feet to spare. Says he could see the snow below him. Well, now the de-icer seems better and anyway there's no big mountains between here and Kimpo, so I guess we'll make it."

The very drunk G.I. sat up in his vomit on the floor and said: "Roarin' and lurchin' and roarin' and rollin' . . ." He waved his hand and appeared to go to sleep.

The sober G.I. looked about ten years older than when he climbed into the plane, and that, I think, is how I looked.

After that we began to sink slowly towards Kimpo with the engines murmuring, 'woom-woom, woom-woom, woom-woom, woom-woom.' The dark man came back. "Fasten seat belts," he said in his efficient voice, parrot-like, and then added as he looked around at us: "Well, if you can't get seat belts, hang on to sump'n', 'cause we're comin' into Kimpo now."

CHAPTER II

I

WE climbed out of the plane to find ourselves in the dark centre of a vast ring of lights. Kimpo's perimeter blazed with electricity and you could distinguish also the tossing flames of a dozen great wood fires. Most of these were burning in oil drums and were so bright that the tiny figures of soldiers warming themselves were visible in meticulous detail, dyed orange in the firelight, a quarter of a mile away. The cold was an enemy you didn't even begin to think of facing: to go somewhere else at once was the feeling into which all thoughts dissolved. We waited a few seconds outside the aircraft for the pilot, though we had no idea what we wanted to say to him. The lieutenant held him by the elbow for a second and said, "Well done, John," smiling. "Thirty hours before I fly again," the haggard pilot said, "so I can get a drink. Let's go get it." "Have one now," I said, producing my bottle. "Yes, go on," everyone said at once. There was a little pause. "Well, thank you," the pilot said, recognising the ceremonial nature of this offer, and took a swig. We passed the bottle round in the blistering cold. That was all the thanksgiving ceremony there was, but it was something. We felt pleased that we'd given the pilot a drink and that he was smiling wearily at us now, with a drop of our whisky inside him.

"Never did like airplanes," the colonel said. "Goddam things."

Then suddenly everybody let their teeth chatter aloud in the wind and cried out, "Jesus, what a country," and fled for the perimeter with their baggage.

8

The 38th Parallel   (*Planet News*)

" Main Supply Route "   (*Television Newsreel taken by Cyril Page*)

Snack-bar in Seoul (*Planet News*)

The Author, with a Seoul Orphan (*Television Newsreel taken by Cyril Page*)

There was a tent marked "PRESS." Inside, in the glow of several hundred-watt bulbs, a number of green canvas camp beds, some of them occupied, were clustered around a stove. I shall describe this stove minutely and with love, because in a way it was the hero of the war. The heroine rather; it was ugly, but I think it was female. You kept coming back to it. It was the centre of all orbits, the preserver of life, the dispenser of comfort, the most beloved object in Korea, and one of the commonest.

The American tent stove then, is a bellied steel pot, like two shallow pudding basins united at their rims. An iron stove pipe sticks out of the top, where there is also a round hole with a cover: a small door in the lower part of the stove reveals a burner and a carburetter, and there's a knob outside the stove which controls them. If you have a jerrycan either of petrol or diesel oil—and what could be easier to get in an American theatre of war—you turn it upside down outside the tent and connect it by a rubber pipe under the tent-flap to the carburetter, light the burner which is something like a gas ring, and turn the knob until the stove is as hot as you want it to be, from tepid to red hot. If you've no petrol or oil, you can take out the burner and carburetter and use wood, straw, paper, coke, sawdust or anything that will light.

This was the homely object around which the United Nations forces fought the Korean war. The Americans were lavish with it. It was the most desired single object of the campaign, and where it was not supplied men would cheerfully commit horrible crimes to get it. In the end it was ubiquitous.

The stove in this Press tent was practically red hot, and anyone within a radius of three yards of it was warm.

It was three o'clock in the morning, but the Public Information Officer's sergeant, who was in charge of the Press tent, leaped cheerfully out of bed to attend to us. He was a small, dark, serious American with rimless glasses, in which apparently he even slept. He had something in his face and manner which reminded me of Salvation Army members I had met or Communist acquaintances of mine, something devoted and unremitting, bright but not humorous. I found out afterwards that he was in love, not with Christ or the People or Marx, but with the Press, or rather with the idea of the Press. And quite a number of the P.I.O.'s sergeants felt the same way. Their ambition was to be a member of the Press, a fraternity they had somehow or other managed to invest with all the trappings of high romance. They were mines of Press lore. They knew just how this or that scoop had been brought off, the biographies of every known correspondent and what the present owners of newspapers had paid for them.

This particular sergeant sat down behind a trestle table, uncapped a fountain pen and held it out to us, indicating a sort of hotel register. "Just your names, nationalities and the papers you work for," he said, "and the date. We like to know who passes through. Thank you. Only two of you? Well, I have beds and blankets for both of you and I can rustle up some coffee in a few minutes. I'm afraid I've nothing to eat. May I say that I am proud to meet for the first time correspondents from the British Broadcasting Corporation."

"Thank you, thank you. Any transport to Seoul tomorrow morning?" asked Page.

"Yes," said the sergeant, " I think I can get you on a truck or a jeep to Seoul City at about nine o'clock. That suit?"

"Thank you, thank you. This coffee now . . ."

One of the recumbent figures on the camp beds now raised itself and sat up, and I was astonished to see that it was a woman: a red-haired woman: parka and boots and trousers and all, but a woman right enough.

"Hello," she said with a foreign trace in her voice. "You just in? I bet you're cold," and she handed me over a bottle. Scotch. I took a swig and handed it back. She tilted herself a mouthful rather elegantly and went on, "I represent a Danish Agency. This is my husband. Let us not wake him, he is asleep. Are you British? Yes, you are. The news is very bad and nobody knows if the Chinese will stop before they get to Seoul. We have come down with the army from Pyongyang, very fast indeed, and now we are going to Taegu."

10

At that moment the air raid siren started. It must, I think, have been housed in the next tent to ours, for speech was impossible while it lasted. It howled for about two minutes. I was well trained, I switched off the light.

"It is not any use in the world to do that," said the Danish lady. "Please put it on again. Even if all the lights went out, Kimpo is still visible because of the fires, and it's only Bedcheck Charlie."

"What?"

"Bed-check Charlie. He has been over before tonight. Usually he begins at nine o'clock. That is why he is called Bedcheck Charlie. He is a little Chinese aeroplane who carries four or five twenty-pound mortar bombs and drops them over Kimpo. There is one now."

A crash like someone dropping a crate of crockery sounded outside, and then another.

"They are Chinese twenty-millimetre mortar shells," said the representative of the Danish Agency, "and they have so far done no harm at all. Charlie drops them over the side and he is a very bad aimer. Two he has managed to drop on the airstrip, but most of them land miles away." There were three more crashes, fainter and fainter in the distance, then silence.

"There. He has gone home. If you have finished your coffee, let us go to sleep. The sergeant will put the light out when the last plane comes in."

She lay down and turned over. I took off my boots and my parka, crawled between the blankets and was instantly asleep.

3

At eight o'clock in the morning the P.I.O. sergeant gave us breakfast, eggs and bacon, which he cooked himself on the tent stove with his air of quiet devotion. "A jeep will arrive in one hour," he said, "to take you to the Nai Ja apartments. That is where the correspondents are living now. The Chinese are still coming south and we have been alerted. We may have to dismantle the airstrip. Would you care to hear the radio?" and he turned it on.

The Korean war was fought all that winter to the strains of

"Goodnight Irene." In tents and foxholes and ruined mud-houses and on the snowy tops of mountains, when you tuned in the wireless that was what you got, take it or leave it. Nearly everybody took it. G.I.s used to be able to make a kind of mooing noise out of it which lasted them the whole day. It was the hummed accompaniment to every activity. There was nothing gay about it, or even sad: it was dreariness made manifest: several times I thought I should die of it. About eight degrees along the scale on the wireless dial the South Koreans were in the habit of going to war to the rousing harmonies of Beethoven, but I didn't discover that for months. Nobody ever turned the Korean station on.

"Pretty good radio sets, these," said the P.I.O. sergeant modestly, and turned it up until it filled the morning.

4

It was a British jeep sent by 2 P.R.S., the British Public Relations Section. Its R.A.S.C. driver wore a stocking cap comforter and windproof camouflaged overalls above his battledress, instead of a parka.

"Mornin' Mr. Page, thought it might be you," he said. "I wasn't able to bring your own jeep because it's not finished yet. How are all the girls in Tokyo? The Kilroys are all roaring about it being the end of the war. D'you think that's right?"

"Who are the Kilroys?" I asked.

"Flippin' Yanks, that's 'oo. There y'are." He pointed to an inscription in paint on the wall of one of the huts of the airstrip installation. KILROY WAS HERE it said. "Write it up wherever they go," said the driver. "Kilroy was 'ere, but he didn't stay too flippin' long. The flippin' Kilroys, that's what we call 'em. Slimy Limeys they calls us. Fair enough."

We climbed into the jeep and set off through a sort of suburb of crashed planes which lay around the airport in various stages of disintegration. The jeep was an open one, and though the sun was shining and the sky was a clear blue, the cold seemed not to have abated at all since midnight. The moving column of air through which the jeep slid was so cold that its sensation was somewhere on the boundary between discomfort and pain.

I had already learned that my greatest friend in Korea was the string that made an airtight joint between my parka hood and the skin of my face.

The next thing I noticed was the extraordinary skyline. The hills—and they were not much more than 2,000 feet high—were like nothing I'd ever seen in my life so much as the fantastic backgrounds to Walt Disney's fairy stories. They were the most improbable hills, that went straight up and down like a row of spikes or sharks teeth. The whole landscape was white with snow, but you could see, in the foreground, that it was only a thin sprinkling and worn away in patches like a threadbare tablecloth. This was the standard, regulation Korean scenic pattern. Wherever you were in Korea, the sharks-tooth peaks encircled you. They might be close up or far away, but they were always visible and always the same.

The road we were travelling on was the normal abominable Korean road, a set of regular washboard corrugations about two feet across and three or four inches deep in the troughs. This roadway itself was the top of a seemingly endless embankment or 'bund' reared up between six and twenty feet above the rice paddy fields—smooth pools of ice, snow-covered and built in terraces whose edges were bounded by little veins or walls of clay sticking out six inches above the surface of the ice. There was exactly enough room for the jeep to pass a ten-ton truck on this road. We made the experiment several times. The foot of the bank on either side of us was a litter of wrecked vehicles sunk belly up in the ice. We were making about ten miles an hour on the average and it seemed very fast indeed.

We bumped through a small, wretched village. The houses, one-roomed dwellings, were thatched with dried grass and looked at a distance like old haystacks. The queer thing about these very modest mud and wattle hovels was that their chimneys, instead of sprouting from the roofs, grew from low down at the gable ends of the houses, crazy lengths of jointed earthenware pipes like overgrown bamboos badly put together. This was the simplest form of the excellent Korean house-heating system. The fire is made in a grate fixed into the outside wall of the house, and the hot air and smoke wander about under

13

the floor, which is raised three feet from the ground, until they have traversed the house from end to end, and then they escape up the chimney. The floors are covered with paper glued down and are smoke-tight, or should be.

Along the street—littered and stinking with every kind of ordure—which straggled between these hovels, the older male villagers squatted in the cold, smoking long cane tobacco-pipes, and as the jeep lurched past them, a rabble of urchins stood at the salute shouting, "Aw Keh, Aw Keh."

Two tattered flags, a South Korean one and a Stars and Stripes, draggled from a window, and a notice on one house-front said WELCOME UNITED NATIONS COMBINATIONS. The old men wore white calf-length coats, full white trousers, very voluminous and gathered at the ankles, and canoe-shaped shoes. The urchins wore black jackets and American khaki trousers cut down.

Past the village we made a sharp left turn into a wider road where two rows of battered telegraph poles carried top-heavy loads of tangled wires, and came upon a military notice: NO STOPPING ON M.S.R.

"What's M.S.R.?" I asked.

"Main Supply Route," said Page. "This is the best road in Korea."

It was a shocking road, but wide enough for two ten-tonners to pass each other. On every sixth or seventh telegraph pole a dozen wooden notices were nailed: M.S.R. NO PARKING and then LIGHTNING ADVANCE, DANGER FORWARD, NEWMARKET REAR, DIAMOND, NEWGATE and half a dozen more. These were the code names of United Nations units. Theoretically, if you followed these signposts you eventually arrived at the unit you were looking for, at the front or just behind it. In practice, the notices stayed up long after the unit had gone elsewhere. You could get yourself killed with no trouble at all following these notices away up into No Man's Land. Only a few days later I was to demonstrate this truth.

Along the M.S.R. bounded the military traffic. Negroes in ten-tonners slung their great vehicles round the bends in four-wheeled skids and carried their wheels within a perilous inch

14

or two of the edge of the 'bund.' It was a kind of 'hit or miss' driving not much more under control than is a boy sliding on the ice. The drivers had accepted the skid and slide of the vehicles as inevitable, and now they used these motions as part of the driving technique. The corrugations of the road surface had a special effect, too, on lighter vehicles such as jeeps: these tended to be shaken automatically ever nearer the side of the road—the steering wheel stayed in one place and the front wheels never changed their direction, but each short bump shook the whole vehicle bodily sideways an inch or two; and unless the driver continually corrected his direction, he soon found himself with a wheel over the edge.

Driving in Korea was a most unpleasant physical sensation. It didn't matter how you sat or reclined or sprawled, one or other of the knuckles of your backbone was always being subjected to a remorseless hammering. You were stiff and tired after fifteen miles; thirty miles never failed to break up my recorder. A hundred miles in the winter was a feat to be dreaded, and I have seen truck drivers calling weakly through the windows of the cab for assistance, for they could not move but had to get their mates to lift them out of the cab and carry them into warmth and shelter. Any driver who spotted a stack or bundle of rice straw by the side of the road would always stop and set fire to it and thaw himself out before continuing his journey, and drivers used to pad the floors of their vehicles with thick bundles of straw: our jeep was about half full of it. That winter, too, American drivers learned to envy the old-fashioned truck of the British Army—only in one particular, it's true: our trucks were slower, less powerful and altogether inferior in pulling power (there were very few four-wheel drive vehicles among them), but they had one great advantage in Korea—the cab was over the engine and at least ten degrees warmer than the American model.

Page rubbed his face where the wind bit and said to the driver: "How long's the wind been on?" "It's the second day," said the driver; "only one more day to go." And he began to explain the curious laws of the Korean weather. There was a strict rotation of wind and calm: after every two days of ordinary

15

calm, cold weather, when there might well be snow, the wind, a north-west one straight from Siberia, would begin to blow, usually without violence, and last for three days. This wind lowered the real air temperature often as much as ten or fifteen degrees, but its effect on the skin was as if the thermometer had suddenly sunk fifty degrees. Its effect on the human spirit was a curious one: it created fear—a quite generalised fear which sapped every kind of morale. I have stood in this wind feeling so small and helpless that I was ready to cry with self pity. It was such an implacable foe. It never let up. It sought you out and wore you down, it was like being nagged beyond endurance. We were having a very gentle spell of the wind, this cycle, but even now it was enough to keep me squirming, hoping for respite, fiddling with my hood string, longing for journey's end and shelter.

The jeep now plunged downhill between sandy banks, turned a corner, and there a mile away was Seoul City. A long embankment stretched a horizontal of sandy grey across the lower sky, for Seoul City was fifty feet above our level, and above this bank rose terrace on terrace of small roofs, heavily tiled and tiptilted at the ends of the eaves, in oriental style.

A thin frost glittered on the roof-tops, and behind them rose those fantastic peaks, like gigantic stalagmite formations, quite unreal in the glittering sunshine.

We were halfway across the great bowl or saucer of sand through which the Han River flows, Seoul's southern boundary, and we were in a long, slow-moving queue of military traffic now. The wind played low, owl-like notes over the hollows in the sand, and whipped a little cloud of dust and ice particles over the horizon to the west. The driver shifted his hood, nursed his hands and said, "Cor, what a place." The left side of my face was quite numb and paralysed in half a minute, and I could feel that my eyes really were spheres, because the whole spherical surface of each of them was aching in my head.

It was while we waited there that I first saw the refugees.

A curious little procession shuffled through the sand at the side of the track. There were about fifty of them, and the first impression they gave as they approached was one of gaiety, for the women and the children wore the brightest of silk clothes, screaming pink, purple, golden yellow, rose and saffron and acid green. The women carried on their heads bundles as big as baby elephants, tied up in the same gorgeous materials. The little girls also walked erect under bundles proportionate to their size—proportionate according to Korean ideas, that is. I never began to understand how such tiny children carried such loads. Most of the women had babies strapped to their backs, Japanese fashion, with bright silk bands, and the girls and boys of walking age often carried a younger brother or sister. Even children so small as to have to be led by the hand carried their small bundle on their heads.

The men, more soberly clad in the wide white clothes of the country or in dark jackets and trousers, had A-frames strapped to their shoulders. These are frames of wood shaped like the letter A with two prongs sticking forward at each end of the crossbar. On one of these frames a Korean peasant can carry four or five hundredweight for ten or more miles a day, more or less for ever.

Most of the refugee men were old, or so young as to be barely men at all, for the adults had stayed to look after their farms or been drafted into the army. The procession's air of gaiety faded as it came closer.

They were absolutely silent, the refugees, except for the whimpering of a child, who walked on still, desperately, long after his legs had given up the struggle, and the terrible grunt, "Ugh, ugh," which an old man gave out at each step. He was bent nearly double under a gigantic load on his A-frame and walked with a stick. His face was streaming with sweat: he wore the baggy white cotton trousers of the peasant tied at the ankles with a cotton bandage, a black jacket and an American felt hat turned up all round and undented. Every step made his old knees sag and drove out of him the gasping grunt of exhaustion. The children's faces were whipped by the wind until they were as red as polished apples: tears streamed from their eyes, and the little girls' Japanese haircuts gave them a sturdy appearance which was denied by their flat-footed, automatic leg action: it was the gait of the utterly weary.

17

C

The eyes of all the refugees had ceased to notice anything hours before. They passed us slowly, in silence except for the snivelling of the little boy, the desperate grunting of the old man and the flip-flop of their canoe-shaped shoes in the dust.

Three hundred thousand of these, I reflected, had taken to the roads out of Pyongyang alone.

CHAPTER III

WE were queuing to cross the Han River Bridge, and now, as we crept forward in the queue, it came into sight, a double row of black inflated pontoons like rubber rafts, immovable in the olive green ice of the river. We dipped our wheels over the edge of the bank, slid them on to the runways and began the slow crossing—5 M.P.H. BY ORDER. At both ends of the bridge a notice board proclaimed: YOU ARE NOW CROSSING THE HAN RIVER BY COURTESY OF THE SOMETHING— OR—OTHER CONSTRUCTIONAL ENGINEERING UNIT.

The American sappers used to put out these notices even on bridges about ten feet long, much to the amusement of the British troops, whose latest comment on this habit had been to erect a large notice on the way down from Pyongyang which said: YOU ARE NOW CROSSING THE 38TH PARALLEL BY COURTESY OF THE CHINESE ARMY. This joke the Americans felt to be in poor taste and it was not well received.

We climbed the further bank in a series of hairpin twists through the sand and were in the city. We took a road which led between one-storey houses towards a hilltop half a mile away, where we could see office blocks of concrete and stone outlined against the sky which might have been the centre of any utility modern town. Chains of dilapidated yellow trams crammed to the doors clanked past us, and on the pavements groups of children waved American flags, saluted and bawled "Aw Keh, Aw Keh."

There were more flags and banners hanging from the windows and on the house fronts. Stars and Stripes, Union Jacks (though few), a multitude of South Korean flags with their red and blue symbols on a white ground and even occasionally the dim flag of the United Nations. The banners read: WELLCOME

19

UNITED NATIONS. MAKE SPEED AND END. HEART-
LY WELLCOME VICTORY. ALL THANKS AND LOVE
UNITED NATIONS and so on.

We passed another long column of refugees. The M.S.R.,
with its notices and its stream of trucks, turned abruptly left,
but we went straight on up the hill over the snow into the
centre of the city, 'Capitol Corner,' where a Korean policeman
on a wooden stand whistled shrilly on a pea whistle in the
middle of the traffic.

The Capitol, the seat of the government, lay well back from
the road in a large courtyard which was guarded by sentries.
It was a massive building in grey granite, frowning with grand-
eur and with a dome at the top which was, all the time I was in
Korea, covered in wooden scaffolding and boarded over. At
the cross-roads in front of the Capitol a huge banner stretched
across the road between the lamp standards: WELCOME
U.N.C.U.R.K.   WITH   BOUNDLESS   GRATITUDE.
U.N.C.U.R.K. was the United Nations Commission for the
Unification and Rehabilitation of Korea.

We passed through the teeming end of a small bazaar to the
left of the Capitol and hidden in a shamefaced way rather
behind it, a narrow alley walled with open-fronted shops dis-
playing great quantities of fish dried whole into a sort of grey
leather, and platters bearing samples of queer yellow food-
stuffs. One shop's whole stock-in-trade seemed to consist of
brass spoons, and the roadway was packed with a cheerful mob
of Korean housewives in unbecoming Ming garments, unaltered
since the seventeenth century—a very full skirt made of yards
and yards of silk or cotton, usually both, and so high waisted
as to fasten practically under the armpits, a strange little blouse
fastened tightly round the neck to keep the cold out and a short
bolero jacket. Little girls' silk jackets were almost invariably
a wonderful golden yellow, the colour of some kinds of brass,
and they wore black trousers; but mature women usually wore
magenta or green, and at middle age a Korean woman subsided
into grey, black or a very sober plum colour.

The women laughed and screamed as the jeep nosed its way
along the bazaar. Koreans had no traffic sense at all. They

never got further than the stage of anxiety which precedes it. You could see them everywhere in Seoul, standing on the pavements, their faces screwed into a knot of anxiety and resolution; then, steadfastly looking in the wrong direction, they would bound across the road to impale themselves on any vehicle which happened to be moving. The normal course of events then was for the Korean to bound backwards again, roaring with laughter to save his face, and bowing at every bound. During this performance, more often than not, he impaled himself again, backwards this time, on some other vehicle's bonnet. One of them, in Pusan much later, who had thus bruised his backside against my jeep, stood rubbing himself vigorously, his broad pumpkin face beaming with good fellowship; he bowed and said, "Excuse ridiculous activity," bowed again, took a step backwards and was immediately knocked for six by a ten-tonner. The death rate for children in traffic must have been hundreds of thousands a year.

Across the road from the bazaar stood a Victorian-looking archway of wrought iron with a semicircular placard above it which announced: NAI JA APARTMENTS. I never found out why this building was called the Nai Ja apartments, or what it had been before the war. It was a prison-like grey cube with three storeys and an iron fire escape on the outside. Inside it was divided into small rooms on either side of stone corridors. The rooms were Korean in so far as they had polished wooden floors raised a foot above doorway level, which had never until our arrival been contaminated by boots—there was the small recess in the doorway where the felt slippers had been kept— but they were Western to the extent of having radiators and zinc-lined sinks with water taps.

We drove through the archway and the driver tethered the jeep to an iron railing by means of a padlock and chain and removed the rotor arm, which he put in his pocket. "Four disappeared from 'ere this week," he said. "They say its Gooks, but I reckon it's correspondents."

I should explain here that the word 'Gook' applied to all Koreans, North and South, and has nothing in common with any such army designation as 'Wog' or 'Jerry' except in its application. The word 'Gook' is good Korean and means 'person' or 'people.' 'Me-gook' means American person or people, 'Yung-gook' British and so on. No Korean could object to being called a Gook.

On the ground floor of the Nai Ja apartments was a little cold office with a counter. A Korean clerk entered our names and nationalities in a ledger and handed us three blankets each, while a mob of filthy urchins pushed and scrambled for the privilege of carrying our baggage up the stairs. They lived on tips and were making small fortunes and fought each other ruthlessly for each new load of baggage; so rudely did they jostle, in fact, that two of them were shoving me off my feet to get at my kitbag. On the outskirts of the scrum a much older youth, eighteen or nineteen, nervously hovered. He was very thin and starved looking, but for some reason dared not shove with the mob. I clouted the urchin who was butting my stomach, signalled the youth over to me, and loaded him with my luggage. There were cries of anger from the urchins and an ugly movement to dispossess him of my things, so I clouted a few more of them and then, in state, among a throng of retainers snatching and biting, began to move up the stairs.

That was my first meeting with Kim, whom I afterwards employed full-time, becoming, as he said, his "father and mother." His life story up to the time when I met him illustrates some aspects of Korea pretty well. Kim was a South Korean of the middle class. His father had been a petty bureaucrat under the Japanese administration, but had died, leaving Kim's mother enough property to live in a small, respectable way in Seoul, but not enough to provide for Kim; so, because all arrangements are family arrangements in Korea, and because in the Confucian tradition family ties are honoured scrupulously up to fourth or fifth cousinship, Kim was sent to North Korea to live with a rich uncle. He was sent to Pyongyang High School, had finished his second term at the University, when the war broke out.

At the fall of Pyongyang he had drifted south with the refugees and arrived in Seoul to find that his mother had gone south, neighbours said to Pusan, but no one really knew. Kim

22

was starving and penniless. He had no other relatives in Seoul. He drifted into the Nai Ja apartments because he saw the foreigners' jeeps outside, and they spelt riches and security from which a crumb or two might drop. But he found that like all other possible sources of livelihood in Seoul, this had been organised. The Number One Boy, the sleek and smiling Korean in charge of the servants' arrangements, was reaping a profitable corner in such appointments. To take on more staff, he explained, he would have to ask the American sergeant for permission; then there would be the question of an official military pass for Kim. A North Korean, too, by his accent? Even more difficult. The pass would cost Kim 5,000 won (about nine shillings), to be handed personally and at once to the Number One Boy, afterwards ten per cent of his salary and twenty per cent of his tips would go the same way. There was only one low, menial job which did not require the magic pass and that was the luggage boys' occupation. That only cost 1,000 won and thereafter 500 won a day—a mere nothing compared with the profits; the Me-gooks were fantastically rich and had been known to give individual tips of 3,000 or 4,000 won.

But Kim had no money.

Had he no father or uncle or brother, then, who could satisfy the Number One Boy?

Unfortunately, none.

Then why continue this unprofitable conversation? He could get a large bowl of scraps from the foreigners' kitchen refuse bin, heated up for 150 won, or unheated for 130 won. Not even 130 won? The Number One Boy washed his hands of him.

And there the matter would have ended except that Kim's hunger gave him a sort of desperate tenacity. He hung about outside the luggage scrum, hardly daring to open his mouth beacuse of his North Korean accent, assailed with shouts and kicks if he laid hands on any luggage, empty as a drum and socially completely in the wrong. He'd been at it three days when I arrived, and had been sleeping in a parked truck in the yard, wrapped in stinking rice sacks. At the first landing on the stairs I took the kitbag away from him because his legs were wobbling and his breath was short. "No, no. Sir, no," he said.

His life depended on the size of the tip. I didn't know his story then, but I knew starvation when I saw it, because I had felt it myself, so when at last we dropped the luggage on the camp bed in my room I gave him 2,000 won for his dry skin, sharp bones and wobbly legs. He gave the money a most unearthly smile and would have been off down to the rice shop in the bazaar like a flash, but, being Korean, his manners came first. He gave three little bows, though only two are required, and the most Japanese of smiles, said: "Kaw mahp soom ne da," loudly, and then: "Thanks, coming beck," and disappeared.

Kim's English when I first met him was very poor and I had practically no means of communication with him, until one day when he was sitting on the radiator I heard him singing "Stenka Razin."

"Do you speak Russian?" I asked in that language. He did. He had about 400 words of Russian at his command, and I had about 200, so at last we could exchange rudimentary ideas.

I had an interpreter in once, in the early days, to ask about Kim's history. What had he intended to do when he went to the University?

"A poet, sir."

"A poet?" I said, speaking very distinctly, for I thought he had the wrong word. They spoke together again for a moment.

"Yes, sir, word, I think is poet. Literary masterpieces."

"Has Kim ever read any English poets?" More conversation.

"Yes, sir. Kim say, all saying 'Shakespeare, biggest poet English,' but say he liking more poet Shelley."

It was all most extraordinary. At that moment, though, all I knew was a vague discomfort at having given a starving poor devil as much as three shillings. "Fool," I said to myself, "suppose everybody . . ." and so on. So when a ragged urchin poked his brutal little face in at the door, I was rough with him. "Go away," I yelled at the top of my voice. He handed me a dirty piece of paper and stood beaming. "An Kiu's Victory Dance Hall," I read. "Fifty Lovely Girls Wait You." There was a picture, too, of one of the girls stark naked, lying on her stomach on a cushion, in what was doubtless an old Korean dancing position. I should have called her succulent rather than lovely.

"O.K.," I said, and the urchin moved off as an American correspondent put his head in at the door. He was one of the group who had started out from Tokyo with us and stopped the night at Taegu. He was wearing the full panoply of an American correspondent, cartridge belts and a huge automatic in a gangster's shoulder holster.

"How did you do in the airplane?"

I told him.

"Well," he said, "it wasn't any worse than my trip. I'll tell you. I got out of bed early and went to the airstrip and impressed the P.I.O. sergeant. Biggest circulation in the United States of America, I said, and a by-line daily. I impressed him with I wanted a plane. Not any time. Now. Boy, he certainly was impressed. 'I got you one right here, Mr. Lessingham,' he said, and he hustled me into one of those two-tailed jobs with the door at the back. A flying box-car. Boy, it was full of 500-lb. bombs, but I'd no time to complain because we took off while I was still rolling about on 'em. They hadn't shut the door at the back and it was pretty cold. I grabbed some bomb fins and held on tight in case I rolled out the back. Well, we'd been going just about two minutes, I guess, when one of the engines packed up—just cut right out—and a guy comes squealing out of the front end. 'Roll these bombs out the back, feller,' he roars, 'we're gonna hit the mountain.' Work? I worked. I rolled the goddam things out the back so quick, I'm not sure at one time I wasn't carrying five of 'em. Well, we circled round and kinda landed kinda on one wing, but safe. I rolled out the back. There's the P.I.O. sergeant: 'Jeez, Mr. Lessingham,' he says, 'Jeez, that's bad, seein' how important your story is. Look,' he says, 'I can put you in another one right away.' He runs me neck and crop across the strip and kinda hurls me in at the back of another of these box-cars. 'Remember me when you get back to your paper, Mr. Lessingham,' he screams. Then we took off. D'you know what that box-car was full of?—500-lb. bombs. Wait a minute. I ain't finished."

Mr. Lessingham sat down on my bed and took a deep draught from a bottle of Bourbon, which he then handed to me.

"We landed at Suwon and as we came in a P.I.O. sergeant comes rushing out over the strip and grabs me. 'P.I.O.'s telephoned from Taegu,' he says. 'I know the position. I held a truck for you, Mr. Lessingham. Press rush,' he says. 'Remember me, Mr. Lessingham,' he says, and he heaved me over the back board of a goddam great truck which takes off down the road like hell. Do you know what that truck was full of?"

"500-lb. bombs?" I suggested, Mr. Lessingham gave me a horrified stare. "No, sir," he said. "Corpses. Stiffs. Horrible stiffs. I been bucketing about in that truck for two hours with a big load of stiffs." He took another long shot of whisky. "Who are the guys in here?"

"Page and I," I said, and I looked round. There were three more made-up beds. "I don't know who the others are."

"The names on the door," said Lessingham, "are Dower, Gordon and Lloyd-Brown. Know 'em?"

"Oh yes," I said, "the Australians. Good."

I was glad to be with the Aussies for several reasons. One was because I had met Alan Dower of the *Melbourne Herald* in Tokyo and liked him. He had a fine record as a soldier and was an adventurous correspondent in the old-fashioned romantic way. Indeed, all the Australians shared this quality. They were good front-line reporters. They believed in getting themselves well into the middle of whatever was going on and writing about it vigorously from the inside. Second-hand experiences and 'think-pieces' did not appeal to them. They liked to be able to say 'I was there.' I might be in for some discomfort if I stuck with the Australians, but there would certainly be stories.

There was a telephone room downstairs in the Nai Ja apartments and another room full of maps where a Press Officer gave briefings in the mornings. I went down to look at these arrangements. The telephone room was a small one with two small cabinets along one wall, shut off from the room by sliding doors of flimsy wood with paper panels. They obscured the telephone from sight, but every word said was plainly audible. I'm told that two journalists, during our brief stay in the Nai Ja apartments, never bothered to go after stories but sat in the telephone queue industriously writing everybody else's, until by the end of the day they had a 5,000-word piece which covered every event on the front and did credit to their powers of travel in a rough country.

There was a queue now of a dozen men sitting on the window seat and on the floor, while from one cabinet came a loud wail: "Oh, God Almighty, operator, don't cut me off again, not again."

The P.I.O. sergeant, a young, cheerful man, in charge of this office, sat erect at a desk. He handed me a piece of paper. "There's no censorship," he said. "Censor yourself according to these rules."

It was the ordinary Field Security catalogue: 'Names and positions of Units . . ., Figures of friendly casualties . . ., Strength of reinforcements . . . etc.,' ending, of course, with the biggest headache of the lot: '. . . . or any such information as may be of aid and comfort to the enemy.' It was this last article which made the whole thing ridiculous. My employers, for instance, would expect me to apply this rule in the strictest terms, but other organisations just wanted the story.

If I sent the facts about the graft and corruption in South Korea, was it aid and comfort to the enemy? It would undoubtedly supply their newspapers with ammunition. Merely to report the plight of the refugees was to do as much.

I talked it over with an American correspondent in the mess at lunch. "Don't worry," he said. "Don't give it a thought. Nobody does. When they get scared they'll institute a proper censorship." They did a week or two later.

When I went back to my room, I passed Kim cringing in the passage by the luggage clerk's desk. "I come up to room, sir, clean boots, run messages?" It had been a mistake, I thought, giving him that money. All the same, poor devil, why not? "All right," I said, but as he put his foot on the first step of the stairs he recoiled. There was an angry shouting noise coming from the clerk behind the luggage desk.

"Are you speaking to me?" I asked him.

"No. Shouting boy."

"Well, don't shout boy, when I speaking boy, or I put you through the window. Understand?"

27

"Oh yes, sir." The clerk hid his mouth politely and giggled. I afterwards learned that Korea was chock-full of bumptious little jacks-in-office. This was the first one I'd met and he made me angry.

We went upstairs. I gave Kim some boots to clean, and he'd just begun on them when the luggage clerk was with us again. No knock, no ordinary little Korean bow. He wouldn't have thought of behaving like that with his own people. Democracy had been a little too much for him.

"This boy not coming in rooms. Number One Boy says," he began in a loud shout, "Number One Boy want to see you."

"Send him in," I said.

"He downstairs."

"Well, send him up."

"He not coming up. He want see you downstairs. He very angry."

My haversack was fortunately handy and stuffed with hard cakes of soap. I threw it at the luggage clerk with all the force I could muster, and it hit the side of his head and bounced off a yard or two. It left a red mark.

"You tell Number One Boy if he not here in one minute, I come down and shoot him. Understand?"

"Oh yes, sir," said the luggage clerk, and shuffled off down the passage.

A minute later the Number One Boy arrived, puffing a little, for he was portly. He came in like a great lord.

"You want houseboy. I find you houseboy," he began at the top of his voice. "Plenty houseboys. This boy not coming here. I say who come, who not come. I going tell captain."

"You insolent, ugly bastard," I said. "Tomorrow I go see my great friend General Pak. He wanting men for army." I had not yet in fact met General Pak, but I had a letter to him and I knew his reputation. It seemed to have reached the Number One Boy too. He had visibly paled. There was a silence.

"Difficult to get pass for boy Kim," he began, modulating to a sweeter key, and shaking his head. "He North Korean boy. Bad people," he added virtuously.

"If Stalin come see me here, you no stop him," I roared. "You small-time, insignificant, mannerless, no account boy. You small person."

"Yes, sir, understand," said the Number One Boy, bowing. "I son-of-a-bitch."

"My friend Pak looking all places for men."

"Yes, sir."

"So you tell luggage man all people come see me here. Understand?"

"Yes, sir," the Number One Boy said smiling. "Regret very sorry," and the insufferable creature bowed himself out.

So that was fixed. I must remember the Pak gambit, a useful acquisition.

CHAPTER IV

AT about half past five I walked out into the streets of Seoul City. Seoul at that time had a million and a quarter inhabitants, of whom 400,000 were refugees from the north. It was bursting with them. Every house was crammed. It is socially impossible in Korea to refuse to receive a relative, and it was a poor refugee who could not find some distant relative to claim in Seoul, or indeed anywhere else in the country. About two-thirds of the Korean people share the patronymics Kim, Pak and Li. To refuse to share your house and food with a fourth cousin three times removed was to lose all face at once, though it was not necessary to simulate any joy at the prospect of providing free board and lodging. Wailing was in order.

There was some regulations (military in origin, to prevent epidemics) about overcrowding in Seoul, and the Korean police were having the time of their lives making fortunes out of blackmail, and their other rackets were doing very well too. Black marketeers were flourishing on the material thrown away in the retreats and on leakages from army stores, and the police took a big cut out of the black marketeers' ventures. They were not doing badly out of supplying destitute refugee girls to the brothels, either, and there were various other enterprises. Middle class refugees, for instance, hired trucks to drive them south. They paid enormous prices, when they were frightened enough, for a seat in these vehicles. The police had the screw on the drivers because most of the trucks were stolen, and frequently the truck drivers were simply bandits who drove the refugees south on to lonely roads and cut their throats.

If there was nothing else to do the police could fall back on the old devices which were working better now than ever.

Denouncing Communists, for instance—a very profitable side-line. People would pay almost anything sooner than be denounced.

So the policeman was flushed with happiness and insolence all over his broad, brutal face as he strutted along the pavements, elbowing people into the gutter, or descended from his traffic rostrum to give some bewildered countryman a great kick in the bottom to help him find his way. Yes, the police were happy, exempted from military service too.

In spite of the thirty per cent on the gross takings which they had to bribe the police with, the black marketeers were in clover. All the refugees' property, which they could buy for practically nothing, could be sold as souvenirs for practically anything. There was no bottom to the American pocket, it appeared. They would pay sixpence each for eggs which used to be a penny a dozen in the bad old days, and enormous fortunes were made out of terrifying brews concocted in Korean barns and outhouses from apple juice, millet and rice, and labelled 'Skoch.' It was usually about £1 or $3 a bottle to G.I.s, and 19s. 8d. of that was profit. It was, of course, strictly forbidden by the military authorities.

But the racket in girls was the most profitable because there was no unprofessional competition. The Korean family custom is rigid and requires a rigorous chastity in women. So right from the start the G.I.s encountered a formidable and unprecedented non-co-operation in sexual affairs. It took some time to dawn upon them that this could be, and their reaction was a bitter loathing of all Gooks. Girls were worth their weight in gold, and there were plenty of them homeless and starving in the refugee columns. An Kiu's Victory Dance Hall probably netted about £2,000 a week, of which the police took half. The result of this situation was, to quote an army doctor, "It's probably the most venereal war in history."

As dusk began to fall, Korean newspapers came on the streets and the city was full of a musical shouting, for the newsboys sang the headlines to the tune of the first two lines of 'Au clair de la lune.' "Au clair de la lune, mon ami pierrot," they sang over and over again. And this catch was ringing out from one

31

street corner to another as I entered Seoul's one modern hotel, the Chosen.

It had all the conventional discreet and stuffy air of a modestly expensive English hotel, potted palms, velvet curtains and all. United Nations officials were billeted there; they always got the best billets everywhere, and as I looked into a small dining-room where the tables were already laid, one of these officials, who turned out to be a United Nations Press Officer, was talking to a correspondent. In the dusk the refugees drifted past the windows like ghosts, the room was brightly lit, the newsboys sang, soft-footed waiters ran in and out.

"No, it's not fair," the United Nations official was saying. "No," he went on, "I don't care what you say, it's a grossly unfair piece of reporting," and he began sorrowfully to read aloud from a clipped newspaper column:

" 'In the luxurious Chosen Hotel tonight, United Nations officials settling down to a four-course dinner watched the refugees through the windows of the dining-room. An unending column, shuffling past in forty degrees of frost.'

"No, it's not fair."

"It's absolutely true," maintained the correspondent stoutly, "and they're shuffling past now and you're just going to have your four-course dinner again. I suppose you'll pull the curtains this time?"

"You imply that we don't care."

"I imply nothing, I state the facts."

"What do you want me to do, not have my dinner?"

"Oh, be your age," and the correspondent flung out.

"What is being done about the refugees?" I asked the United Nations man.

He turned a hunted look on me. "There are twenty-seven of us," he said, "in an organisation called the United Nations Civil Assistance Command. We're not allowed to order anybody about, but only to advise the Korean Government and try to get them to co-operate. What can we do? We shall have finished vaccinating and inoculating a million people in this city in about a fortnight from now. We've organised free rice supplies for refugees now out on the roads going south. We've got a small

32

fraction of them into empty schools and village halls at night and provided some heating—quite inadequate, of course. Look me up here in a day's time," said the United Nations man. "I must fly now. I'm off to Pusan."

"What's happening there?"

He looked uneasy. "Well, I think a good many of us may be moving down there shortly." Then he said, too quickly, "Just ordinary routine, of course."

2

In the bar a young American officer and a top-sergeant were arguing over drinks. "I say finish it now and clear out," the young officer said. "You can't fight millions and millions of drugged fanatics, and it's not worth the waste of life to try. What are we here for, anyway? This is supposed to be a Police action. Bug right out, I say."

"We can fight 'em," said the top sergeant, who had a face that might have been carved with a blunt axe out of some very hard wood. "We can fight 'em, but the boys are soft now. Whaddya expect? They're in the army for the Occupation and some of them are so goddam fat they can't hardly walk around. Most of 'em haven't had to put their own pants on for years: always had a couple of geisha girls to do that for 'em. Four men in the line and eight to bring up the coca-cola," he finished bitterly, and spat.

3

On my walk back to the Nai Ja apartments I saw an interesting murder. The narrow bazaar below the prison-like block of buildings blazed with lights like a fairground, for every stall carried its string of naked bulbs and the multi-coloured crowd surged around the market fingering the goods, while the traders cried their wares. It was very cold indeed, but the wind had stopped. As I stood watching the crowd a jeep came nosing through the bazaar. It had one solitary occupant—a Korean policeman, and he was in a hurry. With the charming manners of his kind, he had already knocked down one stall, one child and one woman, when another jeep, with a young American

33

officer in it, approached from the opposite direction. It was obvious that unless one of them backed the two jeeps could not pass.

The young American sat in his jeep looking around for some way out of the impasse, when suddenly the Korean who was facing him became possessed of whatever devil it is that supplies the power in Korean policeman. He began to shout and gesticulate, his arrogant little black eyes flashed, his brutal jowls quivered with fury, and as the American continued to regard him with a kind of stupid amazement, he suddenly let in the clutch and rammed his jeep forward between a crockery stall and the American's jeep, crashing both of them.

"Oh, why don't they kill these policemen?" I was asking myself in a fury, when I suddenly saw to my surprise and fascination that somebody was going to. For a change had come over the American youth. Here was a situation for which his lifelong addiction to Westerns and pulp magazines had fitted him completely. He became all at once Absolutely Phoney. He climbed from his jeep and advanced with a swaying gait, a small dead smile on his rather silly mouth, and contrived to roll up the pupils of his eyes so as to give himself a dead-pan appearance. He was the Killer in a thousand flicks. For a moment I credited him with a wild sense of humour, then he brought out a tarty-looking pearl-handled automatic and shot the Korean policeman twice. The policeman put his hand to his chest and changed his bellowing to a fit of coughing, then he keeled over and fell forward on the wheel. The youth put his pistol away with a flourish, stood for a moment, hands on hips, the smile still on his lips and then 'turned on his heel.'

It was an elegant piece of celluloid. As he backed his jeep out of the bazaar I could not help contrasting the two exhibitions of barbarism—rather in his favour. At any rate, we were one Korean policeman the less.

4

In the Nai Ja apartments the radiators bubbled and steamed. A crackle of shots rang out from time to time from the dingier quarters of Seoul. Drunks or police, or perhaps one of those raids which were becoming fairly frequent, when a party of men would move into a house, scare off the men by force, firing round them, and then deal with the women.

"Everybody's got the jitters," said Alan Dower to me as though stating the incredible. "They don't want to hold. I've been talking to some G.I.s—do you know what they say? 'I've got my place reserved in the truck,' one of them says, 'and the first little yellow face over the hill in front of where we are, I'm bugging out as fast as I can go. Yes, sir, I'll just wait until one little yellow face shows over the top.' Well, there are always soldiers who talk like that, but everybody's doing it. They all agreed with him."

"Not everybody," I said, and told him about the top-sergeant's conversation. But nerves were certainly worn very thin. The sea-wave assault of the Chinese had scored an initial victory greater than could be measured in territory or casualties.

"Oh, for God's sake," said Page, "let's go up to Brigade tomorrow and get out of this hell-hole and get some sense from somebody."

CHAPTER V

ABOUT fifteen miles north of Seoul among those Walt Disney peaks the road was a loose assemblage of ruts and potholes winding among the bases of hills whose sides were as steep as railway embankments, and covered with a thin scrub of miniature trees affording only poor cover. It was snowing and the sky hung low like a grey army blanket. The Siberian wind had ceased to blow. It was very cold, but the malice had gone out of the atmosphere. Between sandy drifts and broad, dust-coloured beaches, a little blurred with snow, the Imjin River was a black stream squeezed in between leaden plains of ice. A great bridge 200 yards long, struck rigid in the act of tottering, lacked two of its spans, and the Engineers had built a causeway of packed earth and steel girders at its base.

Four British soldiers in stocking cap comforters and battle-dresses stretched tight over layers of underwear, sat by the roadside, 'brewing up.'

"Brigade's about fifteen mile up the road," they said, "coming through Kaesong, and there are no signs of the Chinese: they seem to be taking their time."

"They've go no transport, you know," said one cheerful crimson soldier. "Do it all on their old plates of meat. Wonderful fellers."

"Cor, they must be cold, them poor sods," said another, "all in their little cotton clothes humping it down through Manchuria."

I passed round my bottle of whisky.

"You want to be careful through that village," said the man who pitied the Chinese. "There was a bit of shootin' in there as we come through and there's supposed to be guerillas up here, all around," and he pointed across the river to a group of mud huts just visible through the dark, snow-filled air.

"Right, thanks." We climbed into the jeep.

"Don't 'appen to know no football results, I suppose?"

"Sorry, I don't."

We drove down the Imjin bank and gingerly across the causeway and cautiously through the village. It was absolutely silent. Two young men stood by the side of the track and turned their backs on us as we passed.

About three miles south of Kaesong, there was a 'T' crossroads with a large village strewn about over it. The world was silent. We'd seen no traffic for miles, and there strolling along the road was a British officer, tall, lean and ginger, wearing service dress. I stopped the jeep.

"Hello, Bill," I said, for I'd spent three years in various prisoner-of-war camps in Germany and Italy with this officer.

"Good Lord. Well, well. What are you doing here?"

I told him.

"We're billeting here tonight," said Bill Ellery, "and taking up positions tomorrow about ten miles south of here. Come round with me while I find these billets."

There were already about 100 men of the Brigade sitting on the roadside, brewing up. "The rest are coming through Kaesong," said Ellery. "They'll be here in a couple of hours—I've got to hurry. There's a church somewhere, I'm told."

Past a minute post office with a fly-blown notice on the window, 'Telephone the World here,' we walked up a narrow lane between mud walls until we found a wooden house three times the size of the others, tiled roof, tiptilted eaves, just the same as any other Korean house to look at. On the wall a dozen cat skins, bloody side outwards, were nailed up to dry. The Koreans used them for making earpads, like headphones made of fur.

It was the church. The intricate looking Korean facade concealed only one large room. The floor, raised eighteen inches to accommodate the heating system, was covered in the usual way with black paper to seal off the smoke from below. There was a little altar in lacquer and gilt and the walls and ceiling were papered in dark blue with a tiny pattern of golden flowers. There was no floor furniture except a very old harmonium, made in Germany.

37

We clumped around for a while, estimating its capacity—about eighty men—and then opened the door to go. A child, a boy of about ten, stood on the step outside, scowling and pointing in horror at our boots.

"Christian," he said very firmly, pointing at his chest. "No Christian," he said, indicating our boots. Bill Ellery was plainly embarrassed. We were shuffling about on the paper floor, which already showed signs of wear from our boots, feeling very large and awkward, when the padre came in, a small, gentle-looking Korean in a black cassock. He had very little English. He used no polite smiling, but sorrowfully began: "Soldiers come church?" "Yes," said Ellery. The padre held up ten fingers twice, and Ellery held up his eight times. The padre shook his head sadly, and spoke over his shoulder. Four women came in and removed the harmonium. "Christian," said the little boy, pointing at the padre, and spoke to him in Korean. The padre smiled sadly and spread his hands, then made a motion of taking boots off. "Can do?"

"No," said Ellery, and began a spirited excuse in dumb show. I could follow it perfectly—soldiers might be surprised by enemy, boom, boom, would have to rush out, no time to put boots on. The padre spread his hands, pointed to the paper floor, gave a kind of shrug and walked away from us. "Christian," said the small boy.

"Covering this withdrawal," said Ellery as we walked down the village street, "has been quite a tough bit of soldiering. We've had practically nothing to do yet in the way of fighting, of course, but moving around and keeping the cold out is practically a full-time job, particularly with everybody 'bugging out' all the time."

"No story for me then," I said.

"Well, I don't know," said Ellery. He paused. "Have you ever noticed the way the police treat these poor buggers?" he asked.

"Yes," I said, "big boots."

"Hold on a minute," said Ellery. "I'll get you the chap that knows the story."

He came back with a dark, energetic-looking young officer,

who, after the usual social preliminaries, looked around him uncomfortably, and said: "Oh ,well, it wasn't much." He was obviously anxious to leave it at that.

Journalists who work among British army officers earn their pay. The one thing that fills the officers with terror is the idea of 'shooting a line.' I went through the old routine. "Not writing sensational stories, don't want 'em. Just anxious for background information. No names. Might just fill in that missing piece of a bigger story." And so on, and so on.

"Well, it was nothing really," said the officer, "only the other night, we were looking for billets in a village, and we opened the door of one house, and there were forty or fifty people— men and women—tied up with their hands behind them and crammed into a little room about fourteen feet square. Stink! My God, I never smelt anything like it. They'd been there like that for two days. I was just getting 'em untied, when one of these little police bastards came in, yelling. Most unpleasant little party. I had to kick his bottom for him to quieten him a bit, and I took out my four-five and waggled it at him. There were three policemen, and we put them to work untying these poor sods, and then we let the policemen know that that was the end of their little party. The prisoners drove off in the police truck. Perhaps you'd better be a bit careful what you say, though—oh, astonishing good luck, old boy"—and he took a swig at the whisky I handed him—"yes, better be a bit careful. I don't know what the rights and wrongs are, but it's quite bad enough as it is, trying to explain to the chaps just why we're in Korea gettin' our toes frozen off in this dump, without having to give out that muckers like that are on our side, I mean to say."

This was the beginning of the story of the "Horrible Executions" which was to plaster fat headlines across the world's press a few days later.

For some reason, as I stood looking back down the dark, snow-filled road towards the silent villages where the guerillas lurked, and listened to this simple story, I was warmed and cheered. I felt about ten years younger because it had never occurred to this officer that there was any other course of action open to him but to untie the prisoners and let them go. I realised all at once that this action was quite shocking in the Korean atmosphere, where the cold, the misery of the refugees, the policemen, the aloof peaks, the dark and secret alleys in the city ,the hopelessness and the pervading apprehension of defeat conspired together to make all pain and evil seem inevitable. The spirit of the 'bug-out' was part of the Korean fabric.

I ate pork and beans from a mess tin balanced on the bonnet of a jeep, while Ellery gave me the new positions which the Brigade was to occupy; then we set the nose of the jeep towards Seoul.

In the dark afternoon a refugee child in rags leaned against the wall of a house in the village by the Imjin and wailed weakly. He was a stray. The people in the house sat tight and hoped he would go away: it would be fatal to open the door. They would have him for life, and he was no relative of theirs. We did nothing either, we pushed on.

CHAPTER VI

At dawn Padre Blaisdell dressed himself in the little icy room at the top of the orphanage in Seoul. He put on his parka and an extra sweater, for the Siberian wind was fluting in the corners of the big grey barrack of the school which he had shamed the Government into lending him. The water in his basin was solid ice. His fifty-fourth and last Dawn Patrol was going to be an exceptionally unpleasant one.

His boots clicked along the stone flags in the freezing passages which led to the main door. The truck was waiting, and on the snow-covered gravel in the yellow-grey light of sunrise the two Korean nurses stood as usual, ready for duty—pig-tailed adolescents, their moon faces as passive and kindly as cows'.

They climbed into the truck and gave the driver his instructions. Down University Street and along the tram lines to the portentous South Gate, six tiled roofs high and solid as a fort; along Black Market Alley and down towards the river through the silent city where the first groups of refugees were only now beginning to stir, gathering their wraps and bundles about them for the day's trek.

By the time he reached Riverside Road the padre had passed through the normal first stage of reaction to the wind, that daily renewed indignation that so much malice could exist: he was content now in his open vehicle to lie back and admire the effortless skill of the wind's razor as it slashed him to the bone.

There's a dingy alley off Riverside Street, narrow, and strewn with trodden straw and refuse which would stink if the cold allowed it life enough. This alley leads to the arches of the railway bridge across the Han River. At the entrance to the alley, one of Seoul's slum-dwellers, a woman, tired, dilapidated and old at twenty-eight, stood waiting for the truck. She was a unit in the padre's intelligence corps, and when she had given her information to the nurses, she received 500 won—one shilling. She had risen at dawn and waited half an hour in the wind for this fee.

The truck's wheels crackled over the frozen ordure in the alley, passed from it down a sandy track and halted at the second arch of the bridge; it was boarded up on the far side, and in front of the boarding lay a pile of filthy rice sacks, clotted with dirt and stiff as boards. The padre removed the top four layers of the pile and revealed a terrible sight.

It was a child, practically naked and covered with filth. It lay in a pile of its own excrement in a sort of nest it had scratched out among the rice sacks. Hardly able to raise itself on an elbow, it still had energy enough to draw back cracked lips from bleeding gums and snarl and spit at the padre like an angry kitten. Its neck was not much thicker than a broom handle and it had the enormous pot-belly of starvation. With its inadequate neck and huge goggle eyes, it looked like some frightful fledgling disturbed in the nest.

Gingerly handling this appalling object, which continued weakly to scratch and bite, though it uttered no sound, the padre advanced with it in his arms towards the truck. There, the Korean nurses wrapped it in blankets and contrived to get it to swallow a little warm milk which they poured from a vacuum flask. Then the padre gave the truck driver another address, and the Dawn Patrol moved off to another assignation.

At eleven o'clock that morning, when the padre returned to the orphanage, his truck was full.

"They are the real victims of the war," the padre said in his careful, diffident, colourless voice. "Nine-tenths of them were lost or abandoned in the refugee columns. No one will take them in unless they are relations, and we have 800 of these children at the orphanage. Usually they recover in quite a short time, but the bad cases tend to become very silent children, even when they have grown sturdy again. They don't care to mix with the others. I have a little boy who has said nothing for three months now but 'Yes' and 'No.'"

Korea had entirely reconstructed Padre Blaisdell. He had been doing the ordinary job of an army chaplain until the day when his unit had had to leave behind their Korean mascot—a stray child such as was picked up at one time or another by every unit in Korea, overfed and utterly spoiled by the soldiers. This boy, when the time came for him to leave his indulgent foster-parents, the G.I.s, had been terror-stricken. Screaming and trembling, he had been removed by a Korean couple whom the G.I.s were paying to look after him. The scene had lit a small fire in the padre, which in a few weeks was to consume him. He became obsessed by the fate of the children. He would go out on roads and watch the refugee columns for hours. He tried to talk to them through interpreters. He formed associations with chaplains of the air force and the navy. Finally, he abandoned other work to save the children. He suddenly became an irresistible force, sparing neither himself nor anybody else. The United Nations authorities capitulated to him first. He flew about the country organising collections from Service messes and canteens. Money rolled in and food and clothes. Soon he was bullying the Korean Government for an orphanage and a rice ration. He got both. He enlisted help among the Koreans, and combed Seoul for the lost children, and soon his fame spread even among the villages, and conservative farmers in their grass-thatched huts among the mountains would travel by ox cart into town with strays they had picked up in the ice-bound ditches around their fields.

This was the padre's fifty-fourth Dawn Patrol and it would be the last, for the Chinese were now only fifteen miles away and the air of Seoul City was shaken nightly by artillery fire—it was time to evacuate the orphans.

Outrageous bullying on the part of this diffident tyrant of a padre had produced a promise that a Korean Government ship would put in at Inchon, the port for Seoul, and take off all the orphans to the south coast island of Cheju Do: inexorable pressure had convinced the local commander of an American army unit that he had nothing better to do with twenty trucks and drivers than ferry the orphans from their barracks to the port of Inchon.

All this was due to happen the next morning, and already the nurses and Korean porters were humping great loads of food and blankets from the store rooms into the passages whence the files of orphans could transport them piecemeal to the trucks.

2

Page and I went up early next morning to the orphanage to see them off. It was snowing hard, for the Siberian wind had stopped and the churring of the wind-screen wipers of a line of army trucks which squatted on the gravel outside the building made the only sound in the world except for the very faintest reverberation from the guns to the north.

The orphans, divided into a half-dozen groups according to age, were sitting in their rooms round the sultry American tent stoves whose pipes led out of the windows. They were all dressed up for the journey in cut-down battle tunics, red and white football stockings, shirts, scarves, men's long-john pants and every variety of odd garment. They were merry enough, except in the hospital ward, which I couldn't stand for more than a minute or two. This was the home of the latest arrivals, the silent ones who stared ahead or knuckled with minute fists a perpetual belly-ache, of the little boy who held his hand across his eyes all day except at meal-times, of the girl who had said nothing for a month but, mechanically, every two minutes: "I'm cold: I'm hungry."

When all was ready they filed down the passages clasping rag dolls and balls made of string and rice straw, singing the brighter hymns with hilarious gusto. Korean children are disciplined to perform tasks much earlier than ours. A little girl of four is perfectly competent to look after her brother of two: she can wash him, change his shoes, dress him and be altogether responsible for him, and in these columns of children, responsibility was graded right down to the toddlers. Even a tot of two years old had something to take care of.

The nurses bundled them into the trucks, climbed in themselves, two to a truck, and arranged the clean rice straw mats like umbrellas over each cluster of heads. Each orphan sat on

44

his own little refugee's bundle. They set off into the snow, piping "Jesus loves me" with remarkable spirit and vigour.

I had a few words with the padre. "Suppose the ship doesn't arrive at Inchon?" I asked.

"Then I shall stay in Inchon until it does."

"But there's nothing left of Inchon. It's all ruined."

"There are people there. They will help. Very few people are really bad," said the padre; "they need reminding, that's all. Given a few reminders, they will help. If necessary, we will camp in the ruins. We can't stay here."

We said goodbye to him as he moved out in the last truck. I didn't hear the rest of the story until months later.

Naturally enough, the Korean Government ship did not arrive in Inchon. I don't suppose Padre Blaisdell had any idea of the number of bribes it would have taken to give the authorities a real interest in seeing that it got there.

They did camp in the ruins, and three of the orphans caught pneumonia as they sat around great open fires at night in the roofless houses.

But the padre still had a few 'reminders' to give out. This time he 'reminded' the air force.

Four days later, a convoy of twenty air force trucks shifted the orphans to Suwon, where they were crammed into a dozen gigantic troop-carrying aeroplanes and flown to the southern port of Pusan, screaming with delight, I'm told, during the whole trip. There they embarked for Cheju Do, and there they are to this day.

But I have yet to report the padre's most fascinating triumph. Unfortunately, I have it only on hearsay. While at Inchon, I am informed, he successfully 'reminded' a platoon of Korean policemen of their better natures to such a tune that they gave up their beds for the orphans.

"They were good men, they were good men," the padre said simply.

CHAPTER VII

I

JUST after Padre Blaisdell's move to Pusan, Page and I nearly 'wrote ourselves off,' as the phrase was, by the second commonest of all the causes of war correspondents' deaths (the first is air crashes). We lost our way.

There are two routes of entry into Seoul from the north, one through the old capital, Kaesong, and the other further to the east through Uijongbu, and the latter is the classic route of conquest—the one Jenghis Khan used, and the Manchus. It is not merely a road, but a whole tract of easy country where the hills are flattened and wide apart and the going is good. Twenty-Seven Brigade—the Commonwealth Brigade—the Australians, the Argylls and the Middlesex, were sitting across this route, and one bright, piercing morning we went up to find them.

We took the north road between the silent, shuffling columns of the refugees, weaving our way through the military traffic along the edges of the 'bund' and amusing ourselves by listing the fancy names blazoned in white paint on practically every American vehicle. They were mostly girls' names, but there were some short obscene phrases, spelt phonetically, and a special class of conscientiously bloodthirsty appellations. We decided that the best was 'Widow Maker,' a very slow jeep whose owner turned out to be a weak-looking man in rimless glasses who asked us if we knew where his unit—the Sanitary Unit—was situated.

We went on and on until we came to an area where machine guns were manned and pointing north, where soldiers were sitting on the 'cover' side of ruined buildings, and we still hadn't seen any sign of 27 Brigade. Wherever the road forked we took the most northerly bend, and a little north of Uijongbu we were suddenly brought face to face with 'retreat' in the old style. The soldiers of the Republic of Korea had very little motor transport, they were infantry in the old-fashioned sense: when they wanted to go somewhere they marched. The mile of road in front of us was full of a straggle of utterly worn-out men, the remains of an R.O.K. battalion which had pulled out after two or three nights with the Chinese.

The leading half-dozen men were walking, and two of them were holding their boots in their hands as they hobbled with infinite pain and stiffness through the snow. Their faces, streaming with sweat, were as red as if they'd been boiled and their mouths hung open. Behind them, dotted along the road as far as the eye could see, were men in extreme disarray, hobbling, limping and in several cases crawling down the road on their hands and knees. Few of them had any weapons, a few leaned for support on refugee women who had stopped to help them. As we moved forward through them, we could see the green-faced wounded lying in the ditches among the tangles of telephone wire and old food tins. It took them half an hour to pass, and then the road in front of us was empty. A quarter of a mile further on we saw a great pile of straw on the side of the road and automatically stopped the jeep to set fire to it and warm ourselves. In front of us the road was absolutely bare and silent. We could see, a mile away at the next corner, a civilian car wrecked on the roadside and shining in the sun. The small, flattish hills glistened like bits of wedding cake. We remounted our jeep and went up as far as the civilian car. The silence was quite disturbing: there wasn't even a refugee. Then, suddenly, there was a sound, a very odd one, in the air. Fyuff-yuff-yuff-yuff-yuff and CRASH! About 200 yards to our left a cloud of smoke drifted away in the brilliant air. I looked at it stupidly: it was nine years since I'd been mortared and I didn't even recognise the procedure. I recognised it all right the next minute though, when Fyuff-yuff-yuff- CRASH like the end of the world went off, it seemed, right under our noses.

"Come on!" we both yelled at once, and we spun the jeep round into the ditch, over the ditch, scrambling for grip on the sides of the 'bund' and down the road faster than that engine was ever meant to run. A third crash behind us, as stimulating as strychnine, got something like sixty miles an hour out of that old vehicle on that barbarous road.

We bounded into Uijongbu to be hauled up short by an American sergeant from behind a very grim-looking machine gun barrel.

"I took a chance you weren't Chinamen," he said, "but we've had three machine guns on you for the last half mile. You're a very lucky pair of guys."

2

Twenty-Seven Brigade had been on the move all morning, and we ran the Australians to earth eventually in a small snowbound plain just off the main road, which they were using as a motor park.

The Aussies, in many ways, were the most remarkable troops in Korea. Among British troops from the home islands, with their tradition of inhibited speech, it is almost axiomatic that the best fighters talk least. The Gloucesters, whose epic performance a few months later was to show 29 Brigade's fettle in no uncertain way, were so silent that they were known (at any rate to the Royal Ulster Rifles) as 'The Gloomys.' No one could have called the Aussies anything of that kind. They were under no delusions about their fighting quality, they talked loudly and they fought like devils. It is a fact that one Australian soldier, condemned to a life of peace on duty at the base in Japan, wangled three weeks' leave and turned up the next day by aeroplane in Hungnam, where the United States Marines were grimly hacking their way through a sea of Chinese in one of the most terrible actions of the war. The Aussie reported to the American commander and explained that he had volunteered in Australia because he wanted to fight, not to sit on his bottom in Japan. Could they give him a job? They did, and for three weeks, he fought with the Americans, overstaying his leave by several days, because there was no way of getting him back to Japan. When at last he did leave, his American officer gave him a short note to his own Australian commander setting forth his soldierly conduct and asking that it might mitigate his offence. The Aussie lost twenty-eight days' pay!

These Aussies in the car-park were the same breed. They were being pulled back south of Uijongbu for a rest, but they were already plotting to use this rest period to form a battle patrol and go chasing the guerillas in the hills. They actually did this a few days later, fighting a strange, romantic action in a remote guerilla hideout—a cave at the edge of a ravine thousands of feet up in the mountains, where they had to climb hand over hand to a position overlooking the cave mouth.

Just now they were in the highest spirits as they prepared great bonfires round the edge of their enclosure.

3

Twenty-Nine Brigade held the Kaesong road, and they were lying in the most desolate position I ever saw in Korea. The Brigade headquarters was in a river bed, a dreary plain filled with wind and ice, and the battalions crouched against the reverse slopes of jagged little ridges to the north. Four miles down the M.S.R., in a queer country of little round hills where the snow lay deep, Captain Peter Windeler had his 'B echelon,' and it was there, early one morning, that the big headlines were born.

Page woke me up at four o'clock in the morning. "Come on," he said, "there's a story. Message from Peter Windeler." The jeep started without too much trouble—we ran it downhill through silent Seoul for 200 or 300 yards, and then we were off through the black night and the thick, soft snowflakes to the 'B echelon' area.

Dawn was visible as a grey patch in the east when Captain Windeler poured out the steaming mugs of tea he had made for us and told us the story.

"What's happened," he said, "is that these police bastards have been shooting a lot of people and I think they may try it on again this morning, in which case we're going to put a stop to their little games. Yesterday morning, about this time or a little later," he went on, "some of my chaps saw some trucks arrive about a quarter of a mile a way over there to the north. They walked over to see who they were, and when they got there, they saw this: there was a freshly dug trench about three feet deep and the policemen were dragging about a dozen

E

people—men and women with their hands tied behind their backs with electric flex—out of a truck they had parked nearby. They made these poor sods kneel in the trench and then they shot them with automatic weapons through the backs of their heads. Very poor shots they were, too, by all accounts. You can ask the sergeant-major about it, he was there and it turned him up: he's not so easily turned up, either. Get your story from him, because he doesn't exaggerate and he'll tell you the facts. I do hope they try it on again," said Peter, "I really hope they do."

Well, they didn't. But the story was out and the British newsmen, who had had nothing but colour stories ever since the Chinese offensive bogged down north of Uijongbu, began to spread themselves. Page and I walked over to the hollow between the round hills where the executions had been done and saw, sticking out above the unwrinkled blanket of fresh snow, three slim pairs of yellow hands tied at the wrist with flex. They had been badly bitten and gnawed by the starving dogs which crept down in the night from the empty villages where the refugees had left them.

That same evening I was sitting in a jeep in Seoul listening to the song of the newsboys and talking to Alan Dower about the execution story, when we saw a strange procession passing by. A column of people about five deep, with what looked like straw waste paper baskets crammed down over their heads, and their hands tied behind them, shuffled slowly down the street, flanked by busy little policemen. The rear of the column as it passed us, we could see, was composed of women, some with babies tied to their backs, and these women were apparently deemed unworthy of head coverings. Most of them were weeping with the automatic bleating tremolo of pure fright.

They marched slowly across the street in front of us, yammered at all the way by the police, and began to mount the steep slope to the civil prison which towers above the North Road, a red brick cube as ugly as a threat.

Alan Dower climbed slowly out of the jeep. "Come on," he said, "it's the rest of this execution story. I'm going to have a look at that prison."

It was the hour before dusk. The newsboys were singing

50

'Au clair de la lune' as the frost tightened its grip on the city. I stood outside the barred steel gate of the prison and suddenly realised that I would give almost anything not to have to look inside it. I didn't want to know any more about the administration of this Republic. We had heard the gate clang behind the column of prisoners while we were still some way down the street, and now, through the bars, they were nowhere to be seen. A policeman on the other side of the gate began to yap at us in a hectoring voice, and Alan suddenly began to shout at him. He was a very formidable figure, Alan, and he carried an obvious four-five pistol, and now he had lost his temper and was using the kind of voice which apparently meant 'Orders' to the policeman. After a minute or two the policeman unlocked the gate and in we went.

A long column of prisoners was marching diagonally across the courtyard inside. At a sharp yelp from the warder they halted and knelt in the snow. What was so dreadul about them, I saw all at once, was that they looked like a company of clowns. They were bone thin, their hair stuck out gollywog fashion, their faces were green—the colour of billiard chalk—and their noses were red with cold. I've never seen human beings look more desperately ill. They coughed and shook as they knelt on the ground, but however violent their paroxysms, they contrived always to keep their eyes fixed on the warder so that they should by no means miss by so much as a split second his orders and intentions.

When we went to enter the main prison block the policeman stood in front of us yelping and shouting and holding out his rifle. Alan pushed him aside without ceremony, and then our boots began to wake chilly echoes in a dark stone-flagged corridor. There was a row of steel-barred cells along the passage. In the first one a woman lay crouched against the far wall, shaking and quivering. Long, gentle moans escaped from her at regular intervals. We couldn't see her face, but the baby tied to her back was obviously due to be released from Seoul prison by death in the very near future: it looked like a very old green monkey and was as thin as a skeleton. The cell was as cold as death.

51

Half a dozen guards surrounded us now with a sort of scandalised indecision on their faces. They managed to edge us along another passage and into a big, bare room where an elderly official sat in front of a stove and behind a wooden stove. It was the Commandant, and it was evident that the Commandant was just succeeding in controlling a murderous fury, but he collected himself sufficiently to call an interpreter, and in a voice of silky sweetness began a kind of verbal chess game with Alan. He asked nothing of interest and answered nothing at all—all at great length. Alan was soon tired of it, and, as for me, I had 'had' Seoul Prison long before. I only asked to be able to get out of it before I was sick. Finally, Alan had done with him. We clicked our way down the passage, across the courtyard and at length the gate clanged behind us.

"Well," I said, and I blew out a long breath, "you got nothing out of him."

"This, my God," said Alan, "is a bloody fine set-up to waste good Australian lives over. I'm going to raise hell."

CHAPTER VIII

I

AND so, round about Christmas, the United Nations armies lay in their freezing foxholes south of the Parallel where the war had started. They lay there, shaken by a resounding defeat, with many of their units decimated by frost bite and respiratory diseases, in a climate where half an hour at a time was the limit of a sentry's usefulness—after that he was too stupefied with cold to be reliable. They lay there waiting for the next Chinese advance, and with every day's delay the cold, the dark, the silence, the tales of horror from the gaols and the execution squads, the manifest poverty and misery of the inhabitants of Korea and the apprehension of enemy attacks in overwhelming mass heralded only by the sudden whistlings and bugle calls in the night, worked upon their spirits. But what undid them most, I think, was the Siberian wind. When it blew, hope died. This period was probably worst for the Americans, for there was in that army a very considerable fraction of young soldiers whose spirit fed on the ideological aspect of the war. They had to think of the Chinese Communists as brutal tyrants, and that the Southern Republic stood for freedom: as the tales of mild and correct behaviour to prisoners and population by the Chinese began to filter through, and revelations of the Republic's festering corruption piled up, these young men were left without ballast.

It was quite different in the British Army. I never met a soldier who cared a damn about the ideological aspect of the war. True, the Royal Ulster Rifles had selected the dirge-like 'Red Flag' as their song for all dangerous occasions, and this habit was misunderstood by many people, but never by people in the British and Commonwealth Brigades. No, the British soldiers, mostly Reservists dragged back for foreign service from civvy street in the most abrupt fashion (there was hardly a man in 29 Brigade who did not have some really complicated home problem concerned with his new and lowered standard of income), filled the air with complaints of the unfairness of life in general, the cold, the country and the horrors of the war, expressed in language of a raucous obscenity, but they kept their fighting spirit, it seemed, in another compartment of their minds, and looked upon their job as soldiers with a professional eye. They soldiered well, no matter what.

The Americans had guaranteed a turkey dinner for all United Nations troops on Christmas Day, and since this was the only focus of hope on their freezing horizons, the men were convinced that the Chinese offensive would reopen on Christmas Day—just to do them out of their turkey.

And it was at this time, when spirits wavered like candle flames in the Siberian wind, and the hopes of the United Nations seemed fated for extinction, that the Commander in the Field, General Walker, was killed.

He was on his way up the M.S.R. in a jeep to pin decorations on members of the British Commonwealth Brigade, when a truck turned abruptly out of the column as he passed and swept his jeep over the edge of the 'bund' into the rice paddy, where it overturned.

A British correspondent who was following him in another jeep immediately telephoned the story to Tokyo, and after that, for a few days, thunderous denunciations and threats rumbled down upon us from the Public Information Office, and when the smoke of battle cleared, we were clamped in a rigid censorship, and all copy had to be passed by officials at Headquarters in Taegu or Tokyo, and frequently in both cities.

2

Then it was Christmas. Baker Coy., of one of the British battalions of 29 Brigade, lay that Christmas on one of the most uninviting strips of territory I ever beheld. From the frozen rice paddy plain rose a small hill shaped like an inverted pudding basin and so thickly studded with the hemispherical Korean

54

grave mounds as to resemble a gigantic mulberry. The wind had free access to it between the low ridges which enclosed the rice plain, and moaned the day long and night long among the long bone-coloured grasses which stuck out above the snow.

Baker Coy. lived on that hill. They couldn't dig in, because it was a cemetery, so they had procured from a miserable village half a mile away a collection of rice straw mats, and with these had constructed primitive tents between the four-foot mounds (in each mound sat a dead Korean with his chin upon his knees). The men of Baker Coy. scooped into the grave mounds as far as they dared to build fireplaces, and the cook had managed to find a ledge of ground between the cemetery and the rice paddy, and had dug his cookhouse well in, and roofed and walled it with straw. They had made a bathhouse too, by digging a cave in the side of the hill under the graves and mounting inside it the half of an oil drum which had been split lengthways. This company had brought a piano all the way from England with them, and they had it perched on the side of Cemetery Hill in the snow, the oddest sight I've ever seen. They had dug a sort of amphitheatre in front of it on the one spot not occupied by graves, so that the whole company could sit there, round a bonfire, on their straw mats, and sing on Christmas night. On the forward slope of Cemetery Hill, where the graves thinned out a little, were the sentries' foxholes, each nearly as deep as a man and with a hole scooped out inside like a short tunnel, at the end of which a fireplace communicated with the surface by a draught hole about six inches in diameter. In these fireplaces they burned straw, and the bottoms of the foxholes, too, were a foot or more deep in rice straw, as were the floors of all the tents.

All was set for Christmas. The turkeys had been delivered to the cook, the straw mats spread around the piano, the bonfires prepared—and then came the tragedy. In that straw community, in the sort of cold where fires made the difference between life and death, the most strict fire precautions were taken: but now the cook stoked up a great fire for the turkeys, a fire that grew hotter and hotter as the morning wore on. The birds were sizzling and browning as well as any cook could wish when all of a sudden the straw wall of the cookhouse caught fire. Rice straw mats are nearly an inch thick and tough and heavy; there's material for a good solid conflagration in a hut made of straw mats. Inside one minute the cookhouse was a roaring sea of flames. The cook fled, leaving in his haste a grenade hanging up inside. When this went off it scattered fiery fragments over the whole straw village.

Baker Coy. fought the flames like mad, and they did manage to save nearly all their straw tents. When, at last, the fire was out and they had time to reckon their losses, it was discovered that the cookhouse had disappeared and the turkeys were incinerated: that the amphitheatre was a pond of black ashes, the piano a charred ruin, though some of its notes would still play. Christmas, as they had planned it, was over.

Now it happened that Baker Coy.'s cook was a man devoted not only to his art but to Baker Coy. itself. He had another, very small, spare cookhouse which had not been big enough to roast the turkeys in, and now the cook came forward to announce that he would work for the rest of the day and the night too, if necessary, to produce the 222 mince pies for which he reckoned he had the material. And he set to work. All that day the cap comforter of the cook could be seen weaving about in his little hovel as industriously as the head of a caterpillar making a cocoon. He toiled and sweated while everybody else mooched around saying: "This is a merry muckin' Christmas, in'it?" and comparing the Republic of Korea to various ordurous objects. They handed round the Christmas drink ration, and this improved matters a little at first, until Private X disclosed to a pal that he had four bottles of the strictly forbidden black market Korean liquor called 'Skoch.' A private party then began.

Korean 'Skoch' is a horrible drink and its effect cannot be predicted, since it depends on the circumstances and the temper of the drinker.

The circumstances and tempers of these drinkers could not have been worse, and as night fell, to the sound of brawling and altercation, Private X suddenly went a little crazy. He lurched to his feet, sneaked off into his own tent and out again and wandered unsteadily down the hillside, over the freezing rice paddies and up the low ridge to the west where a lemon-coloured sunset still glowed coldly. He was carrying his rifle and several clips of ammunition.

He lay down on the ridge and for a time watched Cemetery Hill—a gay island of little fires in the cold night.

It was the company sergeant-major, lying in his tent carefully husbanding a half-inch of whisky, who first received notice of Private X's intentions. Something said 'Cheeoooo' very sharply just over his head, and he dropped his glass and ran outside yelling, "Who fired that round?" The next ten minutes were bedlam. Bullets whistled and zipped all over Cemetery Hill; men stumbled about in the dark, cursing, or took hasty cover behind the grave mounds. All the time, the cook, with saint-like devotion, toiled on regardless, making his mince pies, two at a time. In the first minute the assault was thought to be a Chinese patrol, but only for a moment. The company commander hastily organised a party to bring in Private X, and, in order to avoid his field of fire, they were directed to strike north along the edge of the rice paddy and take him in the rear, 'and don't get yourselves shot.' The trouble was, this route lay right across an unsuspected hazard. It is the custom of Korean farmers to excavate a reservoir six feet deep and as much across and keep it filled all the year round with the human excrement they used to manure the rice crop. Over this patch the ice was rotten: three of the patrol went in.

A second patrol was organised and succeeded at length, after a few near misses, in capturing Private X. He still had two bullets, one of which, he confided in a rambling way to the patrol commander, he was reserving for President Synghman Rhee.

The company commander called a 'muster' after that, to see if anyone was missing after all the excitement, and two men failed to answer their names. After a long, fruitless and exhausting search it was decided to look again next morning.

When the cook got back to his cookhouse after 'muster,' every single one of the 197 mince pies he had made had vanished.

The two missing men turned up escorted by the military police early the next morning. They had been, they said, 'browned off,' had slipped away, thumbed lifts into Seoul, gone to a dance hall, got drunk and fought some American soldiers. They were battle-scarred and bloody, but reckoned they had won.

"I don't mind any of it," the company commander said to me next morning, sitting by the charred piano where he had been dispensing summary justice, "I don't mind any of it, it's all perfectly natural—direct result of a washed-out Christmas—*except* that mince pie business. Now that's evidence of a rotten spirit in the unit: I take a very dim view indeed of the chap who went off with those mince pies. Only wish I knew who it was."

3

2 P.R.S., the British Public Relations Unit, gave the correspondents a Christmas party. It was an hilarious affair, held in one of the rich northern suburbs of Seoul, where the houses are built high up on truncated pyramids of stone, relics of the old Korean fashion for fortified dwellings. Major Tom Laister, who commanded the unit in Korea, was 'on to a good thing,' he said. He had arranged to set up his officers' mess in a most luxurious and delightful house whose owners were moving south. "I've promised to take care of it for them," he said, "as well as I can, and of course it's one of those polished floor places, so when you come to see us you'll have to take your boots off."

"Oh, my God, Tom, in this weather?"

"I shall have pairs of slippers laid out," pronounced the major in domestic mood, "and of course we shall use the Korean heating system under the floor."

We went round to see him a day or two later.

It was a beautiful house. Set on top of its stone pyramid, which was nearly twenty feet high on the north side, it was at once very modern and completely Korean. The traditional heavy tiles were in turquoise blue and there was a sun-bathing space on the roof from which you could see almost the whole of Seoul City, for the house and its pyramid stood on a high hill.

I knocked on the door, and then fell back a step. It was opened by one of the best looking Korean girls I'd seen yet.

She was dressed in a long dark blue silk robe and had a flower fastened in her hair above the left ear. Here was none of that great golden moon face of the peasant Korean, but a delicate and subtle and amused face, full of vitality. She had lacquered nails about two inches long and a wonderful contralto voice. I took my boots off, even with pleasure, under the stimulus of sundry little pats and encouragements fluted sweetly at me in Korean, and then I was bowed along a polished passage and into the very last kind of room I had expected. It was the apotheosis of the Tottenham Court Road. It had a massive mahogany sideboard, Edwardian I would have said, three very rich and overstuffed armchairs and a sofa, a polished oak table, french windows and brown curtains with a bobble fringe. It was, I discovered, known to its owners as 'the Western room.'

Tom Laister was there with one or two more, including Captain Alec Haytor, a humorous Scot who was an officer in the unit, and a few correspondents. Tom was roaring with laughter. "We heard you on the doorstep, Cutforth," he roared, "we were listening. 'Shall I put them here?'" he mimicked in a saccharine voice, and then said: "I want you to meet Prince Li." I looked about. No princes. "Behind you," said Tom. There stood the pretty girl, her head on one side, smiling and bowing. "I Prince Li, I Prince Li, Very pleased," and away he went.

"That," said Tom, "is Prince Li, the last representative of the Korean royal house."

We could hear the Prince fluting about in the kitchen, in a rather scolding, hen-pecking manner, and then his felt slippers pattered upstairs and a strangled whisper came from the kitchen.

" 'Ere, 'oos that tart?"

" 'Oo? Lulu? He ain't no tart. He's a muckin' prince, he is."

" 'Oo is?"

"Lulu is."

"Go on?"

"Straight, mate, s'right. Muckin' prince, he is."

"Cor!"

"What a country!"

It was very quiet in that suburb; all the rich had moved south during the last few days and the area was quite deserted. At night thieves moved stealthily about in the empty houses.

4

And then the authorities suddenly closed the Nai Ja apartments, and the correspondents had to move into the abandoned University buildings where various army headquarters also had their being. Kim had become so useful, cleaning the jeep, making fires, brewing tea, cooking, laundering and running messages that I offered him a permanent job and asked him how much he wanted. He said: "Food, sleep and I going too when leaving Seoul."

In the dilapidated University buildings Page and Kim and I secured a small room to ourselves off the main lecture room where most of the other correspondents slept, and where someone who knew how to draw had covered the enormous blackboard with a most lascivious pair of nudes. We put up our camp beds in this little room which had once been the Biology Demonstration Room, and still contained, on shelves, a few dusty bottles of specimens in spirit. It had a placard on the door which said 'Graves Commission.' We were, as it happened, only to be there for a few days, and we had hardly settled in when some crisis in the flow of camera film from Tokyo forced Page to fly to Japan to argue with some set of authorities there. So for the last few days of the year Kim and I lived in the Biology Room by ourselves. And everybody's jitters grew worse and worse. A good many correspondents went south, preferring not to wait for whatever was in store on the front line, and it was widely believed that the long pause was due to the time it took the enemy to organise an immense air force. It seemed in the end as if another hour, even, of the tension would be intolerable, and still the Chinese held off, and still practically nothing was known of their positions, their movements or their intentions. And the refugee columns grew thicker and thicker.

Every day I went up to 29 Brigade Headquarters—to the square of big vehicles and tents parked on the freezing river bed behind the Union Jack and the Brigade flag. The procedure there was always the same: you called first, ducking under a tent flap fixed to the side of a caravan marked 'Signals,' on Tubby Marshall, Major, O.C. Signals. Tubby was a warm, philosophical soul who liked company and if he wasn't busy he would tinkle the field telephone and call the D.A.A.Q.M.G., more usually known as the 'Ack and Quack,' and tell him that correspondents had arrived and invite him in for a drink. Then we would all sit around for perhaps a minute or an hour or two and discuss the war as it affected the Brigade. We got more sense and hard realistic background information from these two officers in ten minutes than Army Headquarters would have been able to supply in a year. 'NOT to worry' was the Brigade's catchword then, translated by Signals into their jargon as 'Nan tear William.'

"Well," Boris would say in the rather dismal pauses which followed discussion of the United Nations' position, "NOT to worry," and he would raise a glass of Tubby's gin. It was sound advice if you could take it.

The Brigade Commander, Brigadier Tom Brodie, was a soldier impatient for action. He was a smallish, slim, very good-looking man, immaculately turned out in any weather or situation, and so full of nervous energy that he never stood still, but prowled up and down all the time whacking the sides of his mirror-like boots with a short riding switch he carried. His 'signature tune' was "ALL RIGHT, then," barked out at the end of any conversation, and his currently most famous remark had been an interruption of one of those dreary cursing choruses about Korea—"Korea? Korea? What's the matter with Korea? I like it—reminds me of Scotland."

"It's a good job the Argylls aren't in the Brigade," someone said.

5

I returned to the University building half frozen every night, and one night after dining in the Brigade mess I was pretty late. It must have been nearly midnight. Kim was in bed and I took off my boots and parka and climbed into my sleeping bag by the light of matches. I was almost asleep when suddenly a burst of automatic fire rang out in the compound outside. I got out of bed and looked through the window. I could see the flashes of flame bursting into the darkness and calculated that there must have been at least half a dozen men shooting out there. Then came shouts and a sustained rattle of more professional fire from the direction of the gate—the sentry had turned out the guard.

After a brisk skirmish which must have lasted five or six minutes, the firing died away into the sound of sniping, and then there was a scream and someone ran past my window, very fast but with a limp, and squealing like a dying pig. I could tell it was a Korean because of the flip-flopping of his shoes in the snow. He moved across the quad very fast and I could hear the scuffle of his shoes climbing the wall that screened the University compound from a loathsome alley of hovels on the east side. Then there was silence outside and sleepy voices began to ask each other questions in the next room. After a while they, too, died away. Nobody bothered to get out of bed. There seemed to be no immediate danger, so I took a slug from a bottle Bourbon I had in my haversack, and crawled back to bed. I remember thinking what a cold night it was.

CHAPTER IX

I AWOKE very early next morning; indeed, I had never properly got to sleep after the outburst of shooting in the compound at midnight. I'd taken a very big shot of Bourbon as I climbed back into the sleeping bag hoping it would give me that ten minutes of warmth I needed to drop off to sleep, but it hadn't worked. As I dozed and shook between the layers of quilted down, I'd been dimly aware, as in a nightmare, that something new and threatening, against which I could only whimper, was loose in the world and had been building itself up all through the night. The moment I opened my eyes to full consciousness, I knew what it was. The Siberian wind was with us again. The mysterious time mechanism which governs the movements of the air masses over Asia had revolved once more: we had had our two days of ordinary very cold weather and now we were in for the normal three more days of bitter misery. Punctually, at two in the morning, this vast clock had switched on the northwest wind.

In my particularly filthy little corner of Asia, once the Biology Demonstration Room of Seoul University, this process had made itself known only by a thin piping whisper among the rice straws which showed through the gimcrack ceiling, and the faintest moaning in the cracks between the grubby floorboards, but my spirit had taken note of it, half asleep and doped with whisky though I was: it had drawn the right conclusions and shrivelled in the night, so that I woke up whimpering and irritable—a smaller man than when I went to bed. I was perhaps the last of the biological specimens demonstrated in that room.

The shooting in the middle of the night, I decided, had probably been a Korean jeep stealing party, in which case the police were probably at that moment following the blood trail of the man who had squealed. He was unlikely to be alive, I

63

thought with vicious satisfaction, since if his wound had been severe enough to bring him down he must have frozen to death very quickly. There might be a story in it. I was familiar, of course, with the ins and outs of the jeep stealing and 'refugee transport' racket—the only trouble was the censor.

Motor vehicles were worth their weight in gold at that time to the South Korean gangs and racketeers. A stolen jeep would be rushed off to some alley in Seoul's maze of mean streets and swiftly repainted. They would give it a new number, paint out the unit signs and stencil a large R.O.K.—Republic of Korea—on the back and the front of it. No American or British military policeman would ever question the activities of a vehicle marked R.O.K. He would be more than content that the Republic's extraordinary transport system should remain for ever a mystery. If a Korean policeman were foolish enough to make trouble, which was very unlikely, he could always be bribed. Within a few hours of its disappearance the jeep would be in service. It would have a smart driver in a Korean military uniform which had cost two dollars on the black market and would be making more than a million won a day—about £100 or $300 for its lucky owner, who would cram the vehicle with the panic-stricken middle-class refugees from Seoul and Kaesong—they could get twelve of them on each jeep—and cart them southward to Suwon thirty miles away at the rate of five pounds a passenger, or rather less if they were prepared to kneel on the floor or stand on one foot on the running-board. For the long trip to Pusan, the south coast port which was the only really safe place in Korea and 400 miles from the capital, the price per passenger was about £120. Where the passengers got the money is another Korean mystery.

There were two things wrong with the jeep stealing episode as a story. One was that it wouldn't pass the censor, because it reflected discredit on our allies and on their capitalistic republic and thus came under the heading 'Aid and comfort to the enemy.' On the other hand, the censor might pass it, and in that case it came under my own private heading of 'Nasty Business,' for there were by now a great many dazed and shamed individuals in the American forces who had begun to find the cause of all their disasters and defeats in the behaviour of the South Koreans, whose troops had, in fact, broken on several fronts. If the censor did pass my story it might mean that the authorities themselves were beginning to subscribe to this witch-hunting impulse—in which case I was damned if I'd use the story.

So it seemed to be doomed either way.

A terrible thought struck me suddenly, and I scrambled out of bed. A jeep stealing party! I clawed some of the ice from the window and looked out. There, thank God, was my jeep, firmly tethered to a tree by the padlock and chain. The twigs of the little black tree were shaking in the Siberian wind; a pale sun was doing practically nothing to warm the world, and, far away, I could see a stretch of one of the southward bound roads—it was crammed with a barely moving mass of refugees. I felt under the parka that had been my pillow and found the jeep's distribution rotor arm was safe. My boots had been left too near the window and were no more flexible than if they'd been cast in metal. They would have to be thawed. Kim was asleep on his back with his mouth open, snoring gently, and I gave his bed a shove with my foot and woke him up. "Get weaving," I said sourly, as he knuckled the sleep out of his eyes. A wave of nausea at the sickly flavour of Bourbon which hung about the dirty little room deposited me on Page's empty bed at this point. I turned on his wireless set, as Kim scuttled out of the room. It was the news.

"Guns roared as tanks plunged as battle flared again in North Central Korea's frozen wastes throughout last night. Medium and heavy bombers were slicing through cloud this morning to slash ground communications and all along the front United Nations forces bitterly contested the iron hard gound inch by inch against overwhelming enemy hordes . . ." a dictatorial voice ground out, or something like it. The Armed Forces Radio Network had put into practice a piece of democratic theory—their news bulletins were read out by sergeants and corporals. I felt sorry for the sergeant who was reading this piece. It was obvious that he was not passionately addicted to reading in any form, and on top of that the scriptwriter's titanic literary style meant almost as little to him as it did to me. He ground to a halt and then said, "That was the news, which came to you from the Armed Forces Radio Network. The Voice of Information AND Education."

The springs of information having dried up, I waited for the educational piece, which turned out, as I feared it might, to be yet another recording of 'Goodnight Irene,' this time howled out by several heavenly choirs locked in an echo chamber with an organ consisting of one relentless vox humana stop. It was the exact musical equivalent of the flavour of regurgitated Bourbon whisky. I switched the Voice of Education off.

When Kim came back he had another sort of news bulletin which made me sit up very sharply.

"Korean persons all going Suwon," began Kim, spreading his hands southwards to make his meaning clear. "Korean persons saying Chinese soldiers coming, so going." Now this was news. Not saleable news, but a very reliable indication of what was going to happen. Nobody ever knew how the Korean 'grape vine' news system worked, but what was quite certain was that when the refugees suddenly massed and moved they did so with good reason. It is quite likely that true information about the dates of offensives was passed on to them deliberately by the Chinese and North Koreans, for the refugee columns moving south were a terrible plague to the retreating army. They choked the roads and blocked the traffic; North Korean spies and saboteurs and South Korean traitors moved with and in the column, indistinguishable from the suffering, footsore, half-frozen mob of ordinary, homeless wayfarers. Bands of Communist youths marched among the refugees until they reached some tiny village on the Main Supply Route late at night. Then they would act quickly. Every house in the village would be occupied by armed youths, who would, for several hours, impress upon the householders and their families the virtue of silence. Any show of resentment would be a death warrant. And then, an hour or two before dawn, the youths would drive the villagers out along the frozen paths into the hills and quickly build their road block in the empty village. At dawn some unlucky supply column cruising northwards to the line would just about reach the most northerly house in the street before it ran into a withering machine-gun fire, while grenades, lobbed from every wretched grass-thatched hovel along the straggling street, would burst in dozens among the soldiers in the trucks. These tactics of surprise were often so successful that every soldier in the convoy was killed in the first burst of fire.

Whatever the source of their intelligence, then, the refugees were always right. The breather granted to the United Nations forces just south of Uijongbu was over—of that I was convinced; and the second part of the Chinese offensive had already started.

I put on my parka while Kim fished out of its hiding place in his blankets a piece of equipment too precious to be left lying about where it might be stolen—it was one heating element or bar from an electric stove. He pressed this treasure into place in a contraption made of tin which he had wired up to the light, and balanced across its uncertain glow a small can of water. When, twenty minutes later, this began to boil he put in half a handful of tea from the ten-pound canister I had swopped with an American soldier for a bottle of Bourbon. We slopped tinned milk into the brew and shared it between us while my boots took the place of the can of water. Then, by the same means, we took the chill off a large aluminium basin of water and did a little circumspect washing.

Very soon the University compound, which at one time had been divided into sedate quadrangles of grass and gravel, was a babel of shouts and curses as the correspondents strove to start their jeeps, which were all frozen solid. Some lit fires of sticks and petrol underneath their vehicles. The more vigorous laboured with starting handles for ten-minute spells. Dozens of self-starters hammered and churned at once, all to no purpose. Some begged help from Army trucks and were towed. They careered round and round the compound in their dead vehicles, screaming and blowing their horns. I was of this last school of thought, but after being towed for an hour and a half I gave it up and pushed the jeep under a long open shed in the corner of the compound where an American sergeant-mechanic had his headquarters. A kindly old man, he could sometimes be induced to spare five minutes for a suffering correspondent.

"What have you done?" I told him. "Well, it was real cold last night," the sergeant said, "and I guess the water in the gasoline has froze and gummed up the gas system." He took the top off the petrol pump, and with a crimson finger fished out a little cup of ice. Then he produced a blow lamp and played its roaring flame up and down the petrol pipe. "That's a useful tool," I said, with visions of avoiding in the future all the morning agony of jeep starting, "and I bet it would be expensive." "You're goddam right," said the sergeant, "you wouldn't get that lamp for a case of Scotch. And just in case you have a case of Scotch, let's call it two cases." His hard blue eye grappled with mine for a second. It was no good. I was in the presence of integrity.

All the same, the jeep still wouldn't go, and I left it with the sergeant while I begged a lift up to Brigade from an American Wire Service correspondent. Kim came rushing out over the powdery snow when he saw me get into the jeep. "You come back? You come back?" he kept asking. "I come back very soon," I said, "and when I go from Seoul, you go." He seemed satisfied.

"See here," said the Wire Service man, "I'm going to be at the British Brigade for just precisely five minutes. If that suits you, have a ride. If not, don't waste my time, I'm busy."

The road to Brigade was packed with refugees. Gay clothes and desperate faces. The flip-flop of their canoe-shaped shoes through the icy dust and castor sugar snow. Their dreadful silence, broken by the occasional sobbing of a child, tired out with hours of trotting to keep up. Their monstrous bundles done up in silk—yellow, magenta and acid-green. The lovely yellow colour of the girl children's short jackets. The yellow-grey dust lay thick all over them and hung in the air like a bruise in the sky all along the Main Supply Route. Tonight, only a few miles further down the road, the weak would begin to fall out. There would be the soft thud and groan of a woman down in the snow, the wails of the baby on her back which nobody would heed, since by Korean custom to put yourself in the place of a parent is to accept all a parent's obligations:

to pluck a howling baby from the back of its dead mother would be to saddle yourself with it for life or lose all face for ever. They shuffled on past us, sweating and haggard. The cold bit to the bone.

I had just time at British 29 Brigade Headquarters to collect the gist of what went on. Yes, the refugees were right. The Brigade was in battle and had been heavily engaged since dawn. "Everything going well," said the indefatigable Boris, and "NOT to worry. Emphatically, NOT to worry." Yes, they would be covering the withdrawal, and expected to pass through Seoul that night. Eventually probably to Suwon. There was some talk of a mysterious entity called 'Cooper Force.' I had a tot of gin with Tubby Marshall and then the Wire Service man whisked me away.

The sergeant-mechanic had mended the jeep when I returned, and I gave him what was left in the bottle of Bourbon and went to call on the Public Information Officer, a grizzled old American colonel known as 'Pop,' who had some reputation as an Anglophobe. His Anglophobia didn't amount to much more than a constant reference to the British as "those goddam Limeys," who, he said, "got in his hair." He was a decent, grumbling old man who had once lent me a towel and a shirt though I was a goddam Limey: but then, I didn't have to 'get in his hair' much. The B.B.C. would have been as horrified as the colonel himself if they had been made the vehicle of a breach of security, so my interpretation of the book of rules was nearly as rigorous as the colonel's own. I could afford it. I found him standing in the middle of the P.I.O.'s office smoking a corn-cob pipe while a dozen correspondents queued for the solitary telephone. Every now and then some member of the colonel's staff came in, whispered in his ear and went away again. It was quite obvious that the 'bug-out' from Seoul was being planned and equally obvious that the colonel, a picture of bilious integrity, was going to give nothing away. So I didn't wait.

It was midday now, so I turned into the American Officers' Mess for a meal. Eggs, sweet corn, asparagus, all swimming about in an excess of juice so that they resembled a sort of sweetish hash: followed by a gigantic 'sweet' course—the main part of the meal. As I was smoking a Camel after lunch and drinking a pannikin of good American coffee, the man across the table said, "The P.I.O.'s looking for you." It couldn't be anything important, I thought, so I finished my coffee, smoked another Camel and went to the Biology Demonstration Room to tell Kim to pack. I helped him pack for a while and brewed up some tea, and then it occurred to me that I might as well see what the P.I.O. wanted. It was five minutes to two when I opened the door of his office, and was immediately in the middle of a 'scene.' Pop stood in the middle of his office. He was inside a ring of correspondents, holding on to the telephone receiver with his left hand and on to the arm of one of the more volatile French correspondents with his right, glaring ferociously and grinding out his words between his clenched teeth. "Let's get this straight," said Pop, "your man in Tokyo is on the end of this line, and you don't say a goddam word to him that I can't stand here and listen to. You boys make me tired. Men's lives depend on what you say and don't say. If you say a word I think you shouldn't, I'll pull this goddam wire out by the roots. Is that understood? Risking men's lives for your goddam little stories! It beats the shit out of me," said Pop. "O.K.," said the Frenchman. He grabbed the receiver and poured into it a torrent of excited French.

"Hey," Pop roared, and clutched the receiver to his bosom. A small tug-of-war developed. "I shall say what I wish to say and you shall not prevent me," the French correspondent began, but immediately thought better of it. "O.K.," he said again ,soothingly this time, "I speak in English." He began to struggle for words. "Allo. Are you there? Well, I cannot say much now. Big things are happening here. Draw your conclusions. It is a big event. Allo, allo, are you there, allo, allo, allo?" Pop took the receiver from him gravely, listened, and then jiggled the hooks up and down. "Operator," he said in a deep, dramatic voice, "Operator. Operator." He went on for about two minutes and then flung the receiver on the table. "Gentlemen," he said "the phone is dead." It was a good line and he made the most of it. "The phone is dead. It's dead because the

exchange is closed. You can't get your stories out now, so I'm
at liberty to give you a little piece of news. We are buggin' out
of Seoul. The main part of headquarters has already gone. The
rest will begin to move out now. The front line troops in this
sector will pass through this evening on their way south, and
the Chinese are expected to occupy the city a few hours after
they leave. Anyone who's short of transportation and wants a
ride south can enter his name for a seat in the big truck. The
Korean staff, cooks, boys and laundry girls will go with the
baggage by train, which will leave Seoul station at about six
o'clock tonight. We will handle any of your baggage which is
clearly labelled and stacked in the entrance hall. You are
advised to cross the Han River as soon as possible, for the
bridges will be blown up behind the army. That is all, gentlemen. Don't ask me questions, since I have no wish to figure as
the father of all the quotes in your stories. Just quote yourselves.
I'll tell you one thing more, we are going to Taegu."

There was an incredulous silence. Taegu was 200 miles south
of Seoul City. It looked like the end. "Christ," somebody said,
"it's the end of the bloody war."

Still in silence, we began to drift away. "By the way, Colonel,"
I said, "what did you want to see me about?" "Oh, yeah," said
Pop, "I've got a message for you, a signal, handed in hours
ago." He gave me a message form which read: TO MAJOR
LAISTER 2 PRS FOR CUTFORTH BBC STOP HOPE
TO LAND KIMPO AIRPORT ABOUT 1700 HRS STOP
PLEASE SEND TRANSPORT PAGE. Well, I'd been wondering when I should leave, and this to some extent made up
my mind for me. If Page was going to land at Kimpo airport at
five o'clock and wanted the jeep, we shouldn't be able to leave
till at least six, for it was an hour's drive from Kimpo to Seoul.
At about six, then, Page and I would load ourselves and our
luggage and Kim and his bits and pieces on to the jeep and
move off through the night towards Taegu. I didn't much care
for the idea of a night journey on the guerilla-infested roads,
but it would have to be like that. We could probably tag on to
an armed convoy. We had a variety of weapons and plenty of
ammunition. I decided to send Page's heavy luggage by the

71

train to make more room in the jeep, and I was halfway up the stairs to the Biology Room to give Kim his instructions when the most extraordinary racket broke out on the other side of the compound. All the sash windows flew up as one, and voices began bellowing and roaring and baying to each other like hounds across the square.

"Diddya hear the news?"

"Chinese are just a small piece up the road."

"It's the bug-out."

"What are we waiting for?"

"Haul your ass out of there, Murphy."

"Just get going and keep going."

"Well, what are we waiting for?"

"Yeah, just up the road."

"We're waiting on Murphy."

"MURPHEEEEEEEEE! Haul ass."

"Goddam son-of-a-bitching Irishman."

And suddenly everybody was running about in the compound. The engines of two score of trucks and jeeps began roaring into life. In a surprisingly short time they slid one by one through the compound gate going very fast. At a quarter past three Kim and I had Seoul University to ourselves. It was by no means a pleasant sensation.

CHAPTER X

THERE was nobody in the Biology Room, but the luggage was still there, and a pile of folded blankets showed that Kim had been packing not long before. The beds had gone: they were the property of the P.I.O. There wasn't a sound in the building except the faint moaning of the Siberian wind and the 'ker donk, ker donk' of my heavy boots on the bare wooden boards of the floor.

This snatching of the beds so early—by the Korean staff presumably—worried me a little. The Koreans always knew. Perhaps there was some reason for moving quickly. I felt in my stomach the beginnings of anxiety: fear had not yet bothered to launch a full-scale attack on me, but I could feel in my solar plexus that he had a patrol out, and as usual my mind began to work faster—not better, but faster—and I began to go over the facts of the situation that no contingency had escaped me. I felt that any minute I might remember some clue to the general situation which would send me roaring down the road to Suwon like a rocket, leaving Page to get out of Kimpo as best he could. But I couldn't see it yet. I began to pace up and down.

Here were the facts: the Brigade was across the road to Seoul and had been eleven miles north of the city that morning. "NOT to worry." They were pulling 'this evening.' Well, that should mean about six or seven. And, of course, they would break contact with the enemy for their withdrawal and not come out down the road in a running fight. Should be all right until nine or ten o'clock. The Chinese have no motor transport, anyway.

My stomach now began pleading its case: "Everyone shot out very fast. The Koreans have already taken the beds."

"Doesn't mean a thing," I told my stomach (rather shrilly though); "remember the bug-out from Pyongyang when everybody ran yelping out of the city two days before the Chinese arrived."

"Yes, but they must have learned something from that rout: they can't be doing it twice. And how do you know the Brigade has been able to hold the road? Remember the Turks at Kunuri? And they were first-class, too. Suppose the flanks have gone, as usual. Then you can expect the patter of little feet any minute now."

"No guns," I replied, "there hasn't been a sound of firing all day."

My pacing had by now brought me out of the Biology Room, along the passage and into the great bare Lecture Hall. The lascivious nudes still sprawled in chalk on the blackboard, the sash windows rattled a little in the wind, and pale rectangles of sunlight lay along the dusty boards. Somebody had scrawled 'Kilroy was here' in black on the white wall opposite the window, and somebody else had followed up this announcement with a contemptuous piece of British soldiers' obscenity.

'Ker donk, ker donk' went my boots on the floor. My stomach kept muttering: "The patter of little feet, the patter of little feet, the patter——"

There was a faint shuffling sound behind me and I spun round. For a moment my heart stood still, for surely only disaster could wear the sort of face that was goggling up into mine. It was a classical mask of tragedy done in saffron, and tears were rolling past the corners of the empty crescent mouth. It was Kim, though almost unrecognisable. He stood crouched up in his little black jacket from the sleeves of which six inches of feminine-looking wrist protruded, swathed about his lower half in fold upon fold of my old khaki trousers, the most miserable object in Asia. He was shaking all over, and now he began a quavering, moaning noise which went on for some seconds before I realised that it was articulate.

"Oh, sir, we going, oh, sir, we going, oh, sir, we going, oh, sir, we going, oh, sir . . ." and he held his fine hands, palms upwards, in front of him like a beggar man.

74

I had to stop that noise.

"Yes, you're going to Taegu now," I said briskly in a loud voice which startled me in the dead room. I took Kim by his thin shoulders and walked him smartly into the Biology Room, where he slumped on the pile of blankets. In my haversack there was one last bottle, a vile, brandy-coloured Apple Jack, whose light-hearted label in pink and green proclaimed it 'Korea Whisky Very Good.' I poured Kim an inch in the bottom of the tin mug and handed it to him.

"Cheers," I said, and "Chi ass," said the miserable Kim faintly. I knew he would not be able to resist that invitation, since it was one of the 'English Customs' that he'd taken some trouble to learn. "Chi ass," he said, and his teeth rattled on the tin mug.

In about a minute he'd stopped shaking. The poor little devil! No doubt he had watched the servants go, chattering and excited, and not without some warmth of security in their little community, the respected holders of military passes on the train. Safe men. Men of 'face.' And no doubt they'd not been able to resist some sort of demonstration of their superior 'face.' I could well imagine the Number One Boy's insufferable "Very sorry"—only, of course, it would be in Korean: "Ho? You no going? Very sorry. Stay be roasted alive by Communists? Very sorry. No pass on train? Very sorry." And the women, of course, would be giving little screams of delight as the Number One Boy slowly and deliciously drew out of Kim the shameful fact that his foreigner was so eccentric (and therefore face-losing) as to contemplate staying in Seoul after all right-minded people had fled. Then they had been going. Then they had gone. And there was the empty city and the moaning wind. Too much.

All the same, I wasn't his nurse.

"Where is the Number One Boy?"

"Gone sir. Gone, gone. All gone," moaned Kim.

"Gone where?"

Kim gave me a long look of utter stupidity. I could see him thinking: "Gone where? What does it matter where? He's gone. They've gone. Is this foreign devil so grotesquely insensitive that he cannot feel the terrible goneness in everything everywhere?"

75

The foreign devil could feel it. So well, indeed, that it had forced him into a sudden decision during the last minute— that under no circumstances would he spend the rest of what promised to be a sufficiently harrowing night in the company of Kim. Kim was far too potent a reinforcement of the quiverings in the foreign devil's own stomach. Kim would have to be put on the train.

"Number One Boy gone station," said Kim at length.

"Right. We pack jeepoo. Quickly. Everything."

While Kim staggered up and down the stairs packing the jeep, I tore a strip from a piece of rough paper and put it in my typewriter. "This boy," I wrote, and then a row of dots where his name would go, "is a servant of the military authorities in Korea and is entitled to a place on the train from . . . . . to . . . . . on date . . . . . Colonel, 2 R.I.S.B.P. ADV. BASE."

I filled in this document with my fountain pen, making an important looking scrawl opposite the word 'Colonel,' and then began the ticklish bit. No Korean, I knew, would bother about what was on the form so long as it was stamped. Stamped with a rubber stamp, in purple ink, of the right circular shape, and with a date. Well, I hadn't been a prisoner-of-war for nothing. We used to be able to turn out identification cards which deceived German security officers, and it would be a queer thing if I couldn't puzzle the Number One Boy.

First, I unscrewed the socket of the electric light fitting and took off the plastic ring. It was the right sort, with a sharp edge. Good. Then I opened several layers of the clothing on my chest and dug my hands well in to warm them. This was no job for the numb and useless paws one carried in Korea. Then I laid the fake pass flat on top of a notebook and released a loop of tape from my typewriter. Taking great care, I was able to cover rather more than a square inch of the pass with tape looped backwards and forwards, and then I pressed the ring down on top of the tape, screwed it about a bit, and when I uncovered the paper there was a very good purple circle, slightly smudged —but that didn't matter. I decorated the inside of this ring with a circular design of letters and figures which meant very little, using a pencil pressed on the tape. I put in the word 'SEOUL.'

76

In the central space I marked very clearly the date. It wasn't bad. I reckoned it would get by the Number One Boy if I handed him a good deal of 'face' at the same time.

I folded the pass and put it in my pocket as Kim came up the stairs to say, "Jeepoo pack."

2

The first part of the journey from Seoul University to the railway station ran through an undistinguished residential quarter of the city, where the larger stone houses were built on embankments faced with stone fifteen feet above street level in the old Korean 'castle' tradition. In the intervals between these residential blocks the street ran between rows of little wooden shops with open-stall fronts and flimsy sliding doors of wood and paper. They were middle-class streets, remarkable only for their hysterical show of patriotism. Ever since I had been in Seoul these streets had been one of the sights of the city, celebrated for their festoons of flags—South Korean, Stars and Stripes, Union Jacks—and for the artless inscriptions on thousands of linen banners which used to hang from the eaves of the houses: VICTORYSPEED I PRAY, UNIFY KINDLY!, HEARTLY LOVE UNITED NATIONS and so on.

All this was gone. There wasn't a flag left. The street was empty and shutters were locked across the faces of the shops.

Past University Street the road becomes a canyon between eight-storey buildings near the centre of the city. We saw a cat in Town Hall Street, and a little further on four ragged and dirty children (a very rare sight in Korea, where loss of 'face' as a parent is among the more serious shames) were cracking open the shutters of a shop with a wooden pole. They fled at the jeep's approach, except for one shaven-headed, snotty-nosed citizen aged perhaps three years, who stood his ground, gave us an American salute and piped up, "Aw keh."

The big linen banner at Capitol Corner was still tied to the lamp standards: WELCOME U.N.C.U.R.K. WITH BOUNDLESS GRATITUDE. You could hear it flap in the wind.

The sun had declined now between an amorphous belt of cloud in the west, and the snow on the pavements was grey and forbidding. At the first bend in Bridge Street, the great thorough-fare where the tramlines run down towards the river and the pontoon bridge a mile to the south, two women were support-ing an old man who had, that moment, died. It had been a sudden collapse, for their bundles, tied up like puddings in enormous cloths, were scattered in the roadway behind them. They were propping him up against the doorpost of a shop, a very old man with a grey beard, a village elder by the country cut of his white clothes. He wore a little black horse-hair top hat tied with a ribbon under his chin.

One of the women, old enough to be his wife, shuffled slowly round under the weight of belongings tied to her back to look at the jeep as it came up. As I stopped it, she raised both her arms and stood extended like a crucifix for a moment before she let them drop to her sides with a smack of finality. The younger woman knelt by the old man's body in the doorway of the shop. There was nothing to be done. Round the next bend in the road we came upon the little band of country refugees from which the old man and his women had dropped out.

In front of us, dropping down a steep hill, lay the last straight three-quarters of a mile of Bridge Street under a pow-der of snow, and I became aware that there had been for some time past a faint rumble, so indistinct as to be more like a shaking of the air than a definite noise. It was louder now, a continuous muffled thunder, and after another half-minute of jerking the jeep between pot-holes and leaden tramlines, I could see what it was—it was the 'bug-out.' Halfway down this stretch of Bridge Street, the Main Supply Route to the north turns abruptly away to the right, and from the mouth of this street, between tall houses, the stream of military traffic was swinging south to the river, a dark, grey-green stream of tanks, jeeps and trucks, with monstrous bridging and digging machines, guns, troop-carriers and half-track vehicles jumbled together, pouring out and pounding down towards the pontoon bridge. The American troops, packed upright in their trucks or sitting on tanks in their conventional panoply of beards and

78

dirt, stared ahead with tough expressions. It was a big moment in the history of the war, but by no means clear in its emotional implications: dramatically, they didn't quite know what to do with it. It was easy to spot the troops who had recently been in tough action—they had a quite different appearance, tired and quiet, not concerned with drama.

White-helmeted policemen screamed up and down the column in jeeps, cutting out a limping jeep here, ordering and fixing a tow there for a vehicle which had cast a track, threatening terrible vengeance on fast trucks trying to 'jump the column.' The faces of the policemen were running with sweat.

It was twenty minutes before they allowed me to join the column, and I talked to an American officer, whose truck on the pavement was the centre of a swarm of mechanics.

"How far behind are the Chinese?"

"That's a thing nobody ever seems to know," said the officer, who was a Texan sort of type, tall, fair, skinny and slow. "They just seem to turn up in half-millions, anywhere, any time. It's right what Mac says: this is quite a new war, and we've not much idea what to do about it yet. Are you with the British Brigade?"

"I'm a correspondent."

"I wouldn't ask you," said the Texan, "only I haven't had a drink in weeks and I'm cold, but you boys seem to get all the booze. . . ."

I produced my bottle.

"It's strictly illegal," went on the officer, tilting a good draught of the Korean whisky down his throat; "we're not supposed to drink this fire water. Does it kill?"

"I'm still alive," I said.

"No," the Texan said, "speaking of the Chinese, I'd say just now their technique has the boys rattled. But not permanently. No, sir. You're a British correspondent; I'll tell you something. The boys are looking poor now, and they know it, and all this 'bug-out' talk and 'to hell with the war' is because they know it. It's like as if looking poor, they gotta make out they're poorer than that. It don't mean much, but it looks damn bad. I know G.I.s."

The policemen whistled me back into the column then, and for the next five minutes, driving between monstrous vehicles in the deafening din took all my time and attention.

Then, the sand flats at the Han River crossing—the most irritating place on earth—cold deserts of dusty sand, where the wind bit into your face like a dentist's drill and whipped the dust and ice particles, a shower of sparks, against your skin. A single file of refugees, a mile long, was crossing the sand, the thick ice of the river and then the sand again. They moved out of some side street a few hundred yards from the bridge like a file of ants carrying their eggs, and disappeared, maybe a mile and a half away, into a horizon blurred with a white mist of wind-borne dust and powdered snow.

On the right-hand fork to the station they were clustered more thickly, and soon the jeep was slowed to a crawl between lines of plodding pedestrians who didn't turn their heads or make any sound but the flip-flop and shuffle of their shoes in the dust.

3

The station squatted, black and hideous, an island in a multi-coloured sea of human beings. The great black Japanese engine, twice the size of an English one, was already letting off throaty hoots from its whistle, and the refugees had rightly assumed that this would be the last train out of Seoul for months—perhaps for ever. About 10,000 optimists were waiting for a place on it. For a radius of a hundred yards around the station they were packed, squatting in the dust, in their padded cotton clothes, the women and children decked out in all their silk finery—three or four layers of it sometimes. Old men, in their antiquated Ming garments and little top hats tied under the chin, smoked three-foot brass and bamboo pipes, leaning on their bundles. Young men, in Western clothes, stood about talking in high, quarrelsome voices. The children played and cried and laughed. There were little fires with cooking pots here and there, and I drew up the jeep close to one of these, where a very ancient woman, in the rather macabre square head-dress assumed by important Korean old dames, squatted over a pot of rice, stirring it very slowly with a big brass spoon. Her head-dress was gravely rich with gold thread on navy blue and saffron yellow silk. I switched off the jeep's engine, for I could go no further through the crowd, and sat watching the refugees. A few tight, hard grains of snow were falling from the dull sky.

"You are from England?" suddenly asked a soft and beauti- fully modulated voice at my elbow. There, by the side of the jeep, was a strange old person, about sixty-five years old I judged, dressed in one of those fabulously expensive fur-lined Korean silk overcoats. His smiling face was as wrinkled and warty as lizard's skin, and out of a nest of crows feet two very bright and intelligent eyes looked straight into mine with a friendly and—could it be?—a faintly patronising expression.

"Yes, I flew here from London."

"Ah, London. *That* seems a very long way away. En-en-en- en-en. It will be thirty-nine, forty, no, forty-one years since I was last there. En-en-en-en-en. I was at school in England and spent some years at your University of Oxford."

He used a very old-fashioned university accent, with a queer little humming noise between the sentences.

Cold can induce a curious kind of mental dislocation. I had heard people in Korea describe strange states of trance in which reality and their imagination had become mixed. This must be it, I thought, because I'd heard that voice before—it was the voice of my Great-Uncle Charles, an ancient parson, dead these twenty years. That soft, meticulous, scholar's accent: "Common are sacerdos, dux, en-en-en-en-en, vates, parens et conjux," Of course the old Korean was there, but I'd given him my Uncle Charles's voice. Any minute now he would begin to test me on the third declension. No matter. NOT to worry. It was an entertaining dream, let it continue.

"We seem to have left things a little late," said the Old Person regretfully. "I have a wife and daughter with me as well as my aged mother." He said a few words to the crone in the head-dress, and she raised her head from the cooking-pot and inclined it slightly in my direction. If ever a face was born to command, that old woman's was.

81

G

He accepted a cigarette ("Thank you, my dear fellow, thank you") with a little bow, and went on: "En-en-en-en-en, Orientals, en-en-en-en-en-en, such as myself, have a bad reputation for begging. Particularly for chits, passes, official favours, testimonials. En-en-en-en-en-en. Tell me, my dear fellow, can you *possibly* make a place for us on this train?"

"I should think it would be quite impossible," I said.

"You are not going yourself?"

"No. My boy, Kim, is going."

"Lucky Kim. The American policeman will not, of course, en-en-en-en-en-en, allow us to enter the station. If you your-self are going in——?"

"I'll let you know what the form is in there," I said.

"I should be infinitely obliged to you, my dear fellow. I have *very* good reasons for wishing to avoid the Chinese," and he gave a clerical titter.

"I don't think you have any chance on the train."

"If money can do it? En-en-en-en-en-en, any amount ...?"

"I'll see," I said, and jumped off the jeep. Kim automatically removed the rotor arm and padlocked the gear chain. It was a drill.

Kim shouldered his luggage and spoke to the nearest Korean policeman, pointing at the jeep. The Korean nodded at me and moved over towards it. Thanks to my privileges as a wearer of United Nations uniform, it would be safe. We pushed our way through the crowd towards the American policeman at the station gate.

"Ah d'know why they all sit here," he said to me as I passed him, "the train's been full up now for four hours."

There in front of us was the train, and the huge engine was barely visible through the swarm of human beings condensed upon it. Men, women and children, they were standing on the running plate, sitting on the boiler, on the buffers, clinging not only to every projection but to other people who had hold of a projection. The tender was full of them, there were three or four on the footplate itself. And behind the engine, every one of the thirty-four enormous covered cattle trucks, stretching away far beyond the station, was similarly painted with a patchwork quilt of vivid silks. Thirty or forty people sat on top of each truck; there were a dozen clinging desperately above each set of buffers between them.

These were the lucky privileged. The mass fought, screamed and struggled on the platform. Four *gisang* girls, the *geishas* of Korea, sat squealing pleasurably on the nearest coach roof, powdered and elegant among the moon-faced peasant women. A hawk-faced crone sat on the engine's running-board, glowering about her and gripping the hand rail in a grasp that death itself wouldn't shift. (In fact, death itself didn't shift it. Later, I watched that train come into Taegu. The old woman was still on the running board, and she was dead.)

I was fascinated by the sight of an old man who'd jogged up and down the platform at a slow but frenzied trot, carrying an old woman on his back. Frequently, in the press, he was forced to a halt, but still his feet jigged away in 'double mark time.' His eyes were fixed on the train as if it was the Holy Grail.

Under the hiss of steam the prevailing noise was the wailing of children.

At the door of the fourth cattle truck, in his good clothes, stood the Number One Boy, full of 'face' and smiling benignly upon the less fortunate. He was directing some last-minute touches to the loading with the sort of wide gestures head waiters use. A ring of lesser 'boys' stood around admiring him.

I steered Kim in front of me through the press with the five fingers of my hand on his back, until we reached the orbit of the Number One Boy, and then I indicated that he should drop his luggage.

"Well, there you are," I said to him; "when you get to Taegu come straight up to the Press camp, wherever it is, and ask for me."

I took the whisky bottle out of my pocket and held it out towards Kim. Simultaneously, I affected to notice for the first time the Number One Boy, who was looking very suspiciously at us. "Ah, Number One," I said, as if greeting a long-lost friend, "very pleased." I jerked the bottle away from Kim with a touch of asperity, as at presumption, and handed it to the Number One Boy, who, after a few little coy gestures of unworthiness and a gay smile round the circle, took a swig. I took one myself and handed him the bottle again.

"They say the train takes four days to Taegu," I said, "but what do *you* think?"

"Eight days," said the Number One Boy. "It takes eight days, not four," I said to Kim sharply. "Well, goodbye, get in now, see you in Taegu," and I shook his hand.

"Very sorry," said the Number One Boy, barring the way and shaking his head, "no pass."

"Where's your pass?" I asked Kim sternly. "Give Number One your pass!"

"No pass, sir," Kim whined.

"Of course you've a pass," I said. "I gave it you," and, as if in sudden doubt, I took all the papers out of my inside pocket and began to go through them carefully.

"Oh, here it is. Of course. So sorry, stupid of me," I said to the Number One, who was now so stuffed with 'face' that he didn't know what to do with it. Public whisky gift, public advice-asking and public apology all in three minutes. It was almost too much. He didn't even glance at the pass, but handed it on to Kim. We had reached the last obstacle.

"Very sorry. No space."

I can't tell whether this Marx Brothers dialogue would ever have got Kim a place on the train, for at this point fate intervened in the person of an American sergeant, who had some position of authority on the station.

"What goes on here?" he enquired, pushing his way in.

"I kept this boy so long doing my packing that somebody's taken his place on the train."

"No space," said the Number One Boy, spreading his hands.

"You a correspondent?"

"Yes."

"You're the guys with all the booze. . . ."

I handed him the bottle.

"Well, how goes the war?" said the sergeant, inclined to gossip.

"I was going to ask you," I said.

He handed me back the bottle and put his head in the cattle truck door.

"Plenny of space in here," he said, "plenny. In you go, kid."
Kim dived in and I followed.

There wasn't much room. Twenty bodies with their blankets and packets of food lay on the floor, and all the rest of the space was marked out by the patches of bedding belonging to the boys on the platform. "Stay here and make space," I told Kim, and began shoving my way out of the station to the jeep. When I came back I handed over three of my four blankets, a duffle coat which I carried around rather uselessly—it wasn't anything like as good as a parka—and my mess tin.

"What about water?" I asked him, for I remembered those cattle truck journeys in Germany. Kim pointed to a double row of jerrycans at the end of the truck. "And selling food at stations," he said. He had made a little space for himself by squeezing up some of the other boys' bedding, and now he spread his blankets. I gave him 20,000 won, patted him on the back and said goodbye. He was happy, and went through his routine of little bows and smiles with pleasure.

I gave the Number One Boy 20,000 won. "Kim will need space and water and food," I said. "I pay half now and the rest at Taegu." So the Number One Boy was happy too.

4

The old Oxford person was waiting by the jeep. "You haven't a hope," I told him.

"I feared so, I feared so. En-en-en-en-en-en. They're obdurate?"

"Extremely. Why don't you buy a place on a lorry, since you are rich?" I asked.

"All the lorries have gone. En-en-en-en-en-en. It was very hard to persuade the old lady to move. And there is another reason: I am carrying a great sum of money. Many of the lorry drivers take the passengers out into the country and rob them if they appear to be well-to-do. En-en-en-en-en-en. You would not care to sell your jeep? I will give you 150,000,000 won."

"Fifteen hundred quid?"

"I suppose it is. I can pay in dollars, but not quite so much— 3,500 dollars. Not scrip, green backs."

There was a long pause.

"No," I said, "I'm afraid it's impossible."

"Then may I beg a seat for the old lady to Suwon?"

"I can't. I am very sorry. I can't, I have to go to Kimpo."

Kimpo! My God! Page! What was the time?

Four-twenty. Never mind, NOT to worry, Page could wait half an hour.

"The best of luck," I said.

"Thank you. En-en-en-en-en-en. I still have plans. En-en-en-en-en-en. Goodbye, or rather, 'Au revoir,' I think we shall meet again," said the Old Person, beaming and bowing.

Automatically I cast my eye over my things in the jeep: bedroll, kitbag, recorder, typewriter. Typewriter? Where was my typewriter? It had gone. No, it had never been there. I suddenly remembered I'd left it in the University.

I would have to go back. It was no good. I would have to go back. I must have a typewriter. I would have to go back.

Only twenty minutes on a fast run.

5

I let in the clutch and moved out fast, twisting a way through the crowd. The refugees were even thicker on the road, and the single file at the abominable Han River flats still crawled like ants across the ice of the river into the bitter horizon. The roar of the bug-out made the air tremble all along the river bank and swell to thunder at the lower end of Bridge Street, where now a tank lay astray across the road, with its track off. The policemen were still screaming up and down the column like maniacs—up the hills, along the tramlines, bouncing at speed across the pot-holes. The dead old man lay across the pavement, his head and shoulders raised against the doorposts, and the wind was playing with his old clothes scattered in the snow. He would be as stiff as iron already. Left, into shadow, and the thin, hard snow began to drizzle again. On this stretch a lorry was stuck, a black open Japanese five-tonner, twenty years old at least. The driver and his mate were wrestling with the engine while the refugees piled in the back, sat on their bundles in apathy or squatted round the lorry in the snow, so that all could sit while they waited. Magenta bundles against the dark snow. . . . 'If they are well-to-do they drive them out into the country and rob them.'

There was the banner, WELCOME U.N.C.U.R.K., and suddenly, in front of me, in the utterly deserted street, was a boy, running. His face was covered with blood. He had burst out of a doorway and now went tearing up Town Hall Street, screaming at the pitch of his lungs. He had missed the jeep by so little that I'd stopped the engine, and I sat there until his screams and his footsteps at long last died away into the silence.

Time for a cigarette. As I fumbled for them, something moved in the stiff and frozen grasses on the verge of Capitol Street. It was a bird, a tame yellow speckled thrush, with clipped wings. Some refugee had wished not to be burdened with it in the bug-out, and had set it free. It could fly about two feet at a time, but landed badly, falling forward. Two yards away from it crouched a piebald cat. The thrush leapt and flurried. The cat slid six inches forward.

I left them to it. As I put in the clutch four deliberate rifle shots crashed out quite close at hand, from the direction of the bazaar by the Nai Ja apartments. I went up University Road pretty fast, but noticed on a wide wooden door, freshly chalked, the hammer and sickle and AMERICANS GO HOME.

And then my tyres were crackling on the University gravel.

Standing on the gravel, looking around him with the air of a man who had seen many other and better places, was a British soldier.

It was a great comfort to see my countryman, and to relish the powerful aura of normality which he diffused. Even in that arctic compound, in a city rather gruesomely waiting to die, he was cheerfully at home, and no doubt had been equally at home, I thought, glancing at his ribbons, in the dust and glare of North Africa and the slow crawl up the spine of Italy. The deplorable arrangements of the Wogs and the Eyeties had done nothing to disconcert him. Nor would those of the Gooks.

I recognised him as one of the R.A.S.C. drivers attached to the British Public Relations Unit.

"Good evenin', Mr. Catford," said the driver pleasantly. "I bin looking for you. This is Mr. Page's jeep, isn't it?"

"It is," I said, "and I should be at Kimpo to meet him now."

"Yes, sir, well. Captain Haytor sent me down here to collect the jeep and go and meet Mr. Page at Kimpo. He said perhaps you'd like to come up to the billet for a drink, if you were still in town, sir?"

"The billet?"

"Yes, sir, you know, 2 P.R.S. Lulu's place."

"Good Lord, is Captain Haytor up there by himself?"

"No, sir, there's me and another driver and two or three Australian correspondents. We're in a bit of mess like. We've no transport. No wheels at all."

"Here, hold on," I said, "I'll get my typewriter. Have a drink."

"I don't mind. Gets a bit parky—well, all the best."

I fetched the typewriter and slung it in the back and we set out again for Lulu's place. It was not yet dusk, but all the live light had gone out of the air, colours were draining away and it was perceptibly colder: it was going to be a very cold night.

We ran north-west through silent, empty streets, and the houses steadily grew in size and richness as we went on, and their stone-faced embankments grew higher and higher until we found ourselves in the haughty residential area favoured by Prince Li, where experimental steel-blue, copper-green and sulphur-yellow tiles flashed between sad pine trees in gardens set on top of pyramids of stone twenty feet high.

At one street corner a high-tension cable sagged across the road within three feet of the tarmac, and we had to climb the pavement to avoid it. A gang of six ragged youths stood there in a rather strained attitude of nonchalance, looking at each other out of the corners of their eyes as we passed. They carried stones, and one of them made a motion of throwing his stone at us as the jeep went by. From the top of the stone pyramid above them another youth was dangling a sackful of loot on a piece of rope.

"Gettin' very fresh, the Gooks are," said the driver, who had given the stone-throwing lout a long look, " 'ave been all day. 'Course, these'll be the Commy Gooks. Might have to do a bit of shootin' before the evening's over."

CHAPTER XI

PRINCE Li's formal Japanese garden was at its most depressing in the early dusk of that bitter evening. Dark, freezing air hanging about between dark trees and dark stones. I couldn't be bothered to take off my boots this time, I tramped right in on the *tatami*. Alec Haytor was in high spirits. "The guests are rolling up," he said. "I thought you were a Chinese general. Three distinguished Australian men of letters are here already, and more are due to arrive—General Kim Il Sung and the Mayor of Yongdungpo. If you've not already written your memoirs, write them at once, at once."

He opened the door of the kitchen, which housed the atomic-looking apparatus which Prince Li's household used for cooking, and a plaintive voice within announced, "It's naw good, Jock, the muckin' mucker's mucked. It won't go, sir, no how," it translated for Alec's benefit.

Three Australian correspondents, Ronnie Monson, Harry Gordon and Lawson Jessup, were sitting on the overstuffed chairs in the icy gloom of the 'parlour.' I clicked the electric light switch. Of course, no light.

"Hello," they said, "this is a hell of a party. No wheels, no light, no fire, practically no whisky and the Chinese just round the corner. Have you got any grog?"

"Half a bottle of Korean hooch," I said.

The driver poked his head in.

"Well, sir, I'll just get a cup of char and get myself warm, and then I'm off to Kimpo. Are you taking your things off the jeep, or will you leave them on? I shan't be more than about two hours."

I made one of the biggest mistakes of my life. "Oh, leave them on," I said. It was the cold that made me say it, the sheer self-pitying disinclination to move.

"Right," said the driver, and presently we heard the jeep start up and move away.

I never saw it or any of my things again.

Perched freezing on Prince Li's armchairs, in a gloom which slowly deepened into dusk, we found very little to say. Ronnie Monson, a veteran of more wars and catastrophes than most of the rest of us had ever heard of, kept firing off short-tempered sentences, in the manner of an old soldier, about deficiencies in equipment and the general inefficiency of the 'authorities.' He was sitting hunched up in so many layers of clothing that his outline was practically spherical, and he wore an American pile-lined cap squashed down over the bridge of his nose.

"Same old story," said Ronnie, "no candles now. When will they learn? The only valuable things in this bloody country are primitive comforts like candles and firewood and whisky. Have you seen the British Army 'space-heater'? My God! Fortunately, there are only about three in the country. All, of course, at Pusan. Anybody with sense enough to run a carrier pigeon service here would scoop everybody else trying to use these telephones. Wonderful vehicles, and no roads to put them on. . . ."

"Pigeons would be no good," said Harry, "you'd have to train the kur-kur bird."

Ronnie fell for this old Korean army gag. "What the hell's that?"

"It's the only bird that stays in Korea in the winter," said Harry. "It flies over the frozen rice paddies uttering a harsh cry like this: kur-kur-kur-Christ, ain't it cold?"

"It stays here, does it? It must be mad."

"Oh, it is. The trick-cyclist's on to it now."

"No, but seriously. They send a bloody great tank like the Centurion and there are only about two little patches in the whole country where it can turn round or get off the road even. The chap who recce'd this place for tanks wants his head examined. It's at Whitehall where they want the trick-cyclists. Same all through; we'd give ten dollars now for half a Korean candle end."

The door opened and Alec Haytor came in. It was so dark now that it was difficult to recognise him. He knocked on Prince Li's Tottenham Court Road table and coughed im-

91

portantly: "Gentlemen," said Captain Haytor, whom such situations as ours raised to great heights as a dead-pan comedian, "Gentlemen, here is the situation: there are seven of us here, four correspondents, two drivers and myself. We have no transport with us of any kind. We are, however, expecting Cyril Page and a driver to return from Kimpo in about an hour and an half, maybe. Jim Hayes and Roly Herman may drop in, in which case there will be another jeep, and we may be able to cram one man on to it."

"Where are Jim and Roly?" I asked.

"They've been up at Brigade all day," said Alec, "and if there still is a Brigade, they are doubtless with it now, unless they've been surprised by guerillas on the way back. Their plan was to stay with Brigade until it began to pull out and then to come straight back here on their way south. There is some faint possibility, however, that someone will send us a jeep from Suwon, and in the last resort we could walk the two miles to the Han River bridge and beg a lift on Brigade transport as it goes through. That walk might well be interesting. Thank you."

WHOOOMP!

A tremendous explosion rocked the little house and a pane of glass tinkled on the floor somewhere. There was a second's silence.

"Thank you," said Alec again.

"Come on," said Ronnie Monson, and led the way up the little toy staircase to the flat leads of the roof.

To the west and south the city lay all below us in the dusk. Against a yellow lemon sunset the tip-tilted roofs to the west showed in silhouette, and a little to the north of them a gigantic pillar of smoke hung in the sky. There were no lights in the city. It took the cold about three minutes to pierce right through parka and battledress and underclothes. It had just got as far as my skin when an orange flame leapt up on the northern perimeter half a mile away, made a little bright island of brilliant details—a shop front, the upper storey of a house, a cobbled pavement in the blackness and then WHOOOMP!—much closer this time, and the flames spread outward in an orange sea. A black tree of smoke grew rapidly up into the sky.

"That was petrol," said Ronnie, "and I reckon the first was ammunition. They must be blowing the dumps."

A thin crackle of automatic fire reached us from somewhere in the city.

"*Someone* is blowing the dumps," he amended, "either the Yanks or the Commy Gooks. I don't much fancy that walk Alec talked about."

We'd been watching the fires dwindle in the dusk for ten minutes or so when we heard a pair of inexpert feet fumbling their way up Prince Li's tiny stairs, and then a New Zealand major stepped out on the leads.

"I heard you were here, but I didn't believe it," he said; "are you a unit, or what?"

"There is part of a unit here, sir," said Alec, "2 P.R.S., the British Public Relations Unit. I'm in charge here. The rest are correspondents, and not responsible for their actions."

"I see," said the major evenly. "Well, my advice to you all is to leave at once. Things are not looking pretty down there in the town. I don't wish to alarm you unduly, but looting has begun on a big scale, and the Korean police appear to have left, but I think I saw some of them among the looters."

"We'd have gone some time ago, sir," said Alec, "only we have no wheels."

"No transport at all?"

Alec explained. "We have one jeep that should be coming back from Kimpo any time now, but that's all."

The major, I suppose he must have been a gunner, was silent for a minute. No one did or said anything to dispel the air of flippancy which the group had adopted for small 'all-round defence' during the night, but as the silence continued you could feel the weight of anxiety shifting about between us. Perhaps the major would take it on himself, we all privately hoped. Would I be bothered, I remember thinking, if I were a gunner major about my lawful occasions, and busy too? For a lot of correspondents? Possibly. Possibly not.

Another dump went up to the south with a flash and a CRUMP!

"I regard this as serious," the major said at length, in his quiet, even New Zealand voice. "I'm going to Suwon now and I shall send a vehicle up for you. With luck, it may be here in two and a half hours, or I may find someone on the way out of Seoul to come and collect you. Don't underestimate the situation. Good night."

"That's very good of you," we said, "thank you very much indeed. Awfully good of you. Well, that's a relief."

The major clattered down the stairs.

"Have you seen the road to Suwon today?" asked Ronnie of Alec, "because the major will have a lot of luck if he gets through in this traffic in four hours. He'll have another lot of luck if he's even allowed on the road in the opposite direction."

We found out later that the major had, in fact, taken about four hours to reach Suwon. He had started back immediately in a truck. Five miles out of Suwon he'd been shoved off the road by a ten-tonner, and his truck lay in the ditch with a broken axle. He had hitch-hiked back to Suwon, found a jeep and started again. This time, after covering fifteen miles in three hours, battling against the bug-out, he had been policed off the road.

The dump fires flickered on the edge of the city, but there was nothing else to see, so we went back to the parlour. Just before we left the roof I heard, far away, the throaty hooting of a train—that continuous whistling noise that meant it was on the move and warning the wretched refugees off the railway track. There was only one train which could be moving. Kim was on his way.

2

It was black night in the parlour, the bobble-fringed curtains silhouetted on the dark blue rectangles of the french windows. It was both freezing and stuffy. We passed the bottle around—very little left.

It was so cold sitting on that armchair that about this time I went off into that queer, dreamy state that many people reported as part of their experience in the Korean winter. It seems to be a different experience for each individual. Most people describe it as something that queer to 'overtake' them. I used to go out of my way to meet it. It happens when the whole atmosphere, the medium in which the individual lives, becomes so uncomfortable as to be an enemy, and it is a little like sleep in so far as consciousness is depressed almost to the level of sleep, but not quite, because it's too cold to go right off—the ache in your icy extremities is still there, but somehow a little way off—it is a withdrawal of consciousness from the outside world, and in my case, to some extent, voluntary.

If you were quite still, sent your mind wandering gently away from your discomforts, you could achieve a state in which the cold was no longer a matter of urgency: but to achieve it you had to go down to the very bottom of consciousness and occasionally a fraction below it, so that thought and fancy and fact swirled nebulously around in the mind like a sea. Little, hard islands of fact would keep appearing in this grey ocean, and it was essential not to land on them, for they were always painful. With practice the swimmer could always change direction whenever an island loomed up and push himself off into the deep sea again. Some of the islands, though, were unavoidable, and all you could say for the sea itself was that it was slightly less painful than reality; it was somewhere else but nowhere very desirable.

With a little whimper about my feet, then, I slipped into this just warmer ocean. My boots—I could see them, dry cow-dung-coloured and black on the highlights of the wrinkles, and over them would go great tea-cosy shapes of quilted kapok, or perhaps there might be double rubber boots with hot water between them. From kettles. Kettles in kitchens, like my kitchen in London, steaming and hot, with a spot of light on each aluminium lid, like soldiers on the shelf. Soldiers shooting on the shelf, shooting automatic fire down in the city where it was so cold on the shelf. And under the shelf rabbits warm in burrows, hopping with a hopping bird, under snow, a hopping thrush with clipped wings, safe now, or dead now, in no light where it was warm, in no light, no light, no light!

It was Alec carrying a large tin box which he had filled with sand and petrol and lighted. He put it on the mahogany sideboard, a fitful little fire which drenched the room in petrol stink and smuts, and gave out a smudgy red light as an afterthought. It was a change, anyway. My feet, my feet. Don't move or you'll know all about it. Don't move. Slip away again.

For a couple of hours I managed to keep floating about among these Hieronymus Bosch-like compositions in which snow landscapes and shooting and the bright red of blood were constant ingredients. Every now and again the crash of another exploding dump brought me into full consciousness, and I was aware from time to time of a faint but real rattle of musketry down in the city. The next island of consciousness was the voice of Alec saying:

"I don't know whether any of you are interested, but the whole place is on fire."

We climbed the stairs to the leads again, stumbling in the dark.

The wind moaned in the hollows of a stone lantern in Prince Li's garden and whispered in the fir trees. Seoul was burning.

Over the whole of the southern and western perimeter of the city bristled an aureole of crimson light; and nearer, dotted about in the black sea of roof tops which rolled right up to the base of our pyramid, a dozen islands of orange flame grew—one big one was recognisable by the light it shed on the tiny streets about it as an area near the Capitol building, and, like a small moon above the flames, the scaffolded dome glowed pink. Another big blaze silhouetted the Chosen Hotel.

At intervals, now of less than half a minute, the rattle and crackle of automatic fire drifted up to our ears with an occasional closer burst like a racing motor cycle engine in the streets immediately below us. One was so close that in the silence which followed it we could hear the click of a gun bolt and laughter and voices in the gully at the pyramid's base.

Alec, who was responsible for the safety of his unit, kept looking at his watch.

"We'll give these jeeps another half-hour," he said, "and then, if they're not here, we'll have to walk down to the bridge."

In the kitchen a flicker of flame showed the drivers making coffee over a wood fire. They handed it around in fine china cups which they'd found in a cupboard, and we were standing about drinking it slowly in the gloom of the kitchen, constantly besought by one of the drivers to 'mind that bloody gret hole,' a death trap in the form of a six-foot-deep grave which led to the Korean floor heating system, when we heard a jeep. We froze into silence. It was. We heard it stop, we heard the voice of Cyril Page, and then there he was in the kitchen, reaching out his hand for coffee, elaborately casual, pale eyes and sardonic beard turning from one to another of the group.

"Your luggage has gone," he said to me.

"Gone where?"

"Pinched. Possibly burnt. Gone, anyway."

"What happened?"

"My God, this is good," said Page, warming his hands on the coffee. "Well, the driver had to wait for me at Kimpo. Plane was late of course. It's very cold, and he left the jeep and went and sat in a hut with some airstrip people. Had a cup of coffee. When he came out the jeep had gone."

"The silly fool!" I said. "Didn't he even lock it?"

"No, and he left the rotor arm in. Well, there was some idea that somebody might have wheeled it into shelter in an outbuilding near the strip, but they are burning the outbuildings, some of them tonight, the rest tomorrow. Anyway, we couldn't find it."

"Where's the driver?" asked Alec.

"Well, I couldn't get a lift for him," said Page, "so I put him on the plane I came in and he's gone down to Taegu. It's the last plane. They're blowing up the landing strip."

"Thank heaven he's all right," Alec said. "What's it like in Seoul?"

"Most of the fire is in the modern part, all around the Town Hall and the Capitol and the Chosen, and along Bridge Street. There's looting going on, and some shooting."

"Who set fire to it?" asked Ronnie irritably, as if it was his property.

"The Yank police say it's Communist sympathisers, but the Korean police say it's patriotic South Koreans denying the use of the capital to the enemy."

"Well, well."

"Well, I'm going into the town to get some pictures," said Page.

H

"Better wait a minute and see if Jim and Roly come in."

They came in twenty minutes later, talking in low tones to each other, secretive about their story. I would have to get what I could on the bridge, where the Brigade was pulling out. A good illustration, I thought bitterly, of how useless a day without assured transport was bound to be in Korea. I suppose I could have thumbed lifts, but not where and when I really wanted them. Good story, whatever it is, I thought, watching Jim's face.

Page had arrived with a Canadian photographer, and these two now went off into the town for pictures. "Back in half an hour," they said. Roly Herman and Jim Hayes took their jeep, too, for a look at the Chosen Hotel. The rest of us waited in the smoky parlour and packed and repacked our belongings.

It was about midnight when the jeeps returned, and shortly afterwards, after a farewell brew of coffee, we put the fires out in Lulu's place and moved into the street.

3

It was pitch dark and desperately cold. One of the jeeps had a trailer, and most of the luggage went on that. We loaded it in the light of headlamps, and then Page and I and the Canadian and Driver Hoskyn crammed ourselves into the other jeep on top of Page's luggage. Our jeep led the convoy. We waited three or four minutes until the other jeep hooted to show it was ready to follow us, then we slid down thesteep gully between the stone pyramids and out on to the suburb's main road. Ahead of us rows of tip-tilted roofs were silhouetted against a crimson glow. We headed towards the fire. The streets were completely deserted, and for nearly a mile utterly dark. It was a sudden discovery at one roundabout that the whole side of the street ahead of us was dully lit by a red light low down. A minute later, and we needed no more jeep lights, for a brilliant orange glare danced on the house fronts and made the long shadows move in the gutters, and we heard the roar and crackle of the fire. Three men in the uniforms of Korean soldiers or policemen went slinking down an alley off this street, with their rifles held at the ready, and the packs on their backs full to bursting with loot; a great silver cup thrust its bowl out of one haversack and a roll of purple silk was tied to the shoulder straps of another. The men moved off down the orange-coloured ravine of the alley, warily, like prowling cats, in single file.

In University Road a quarter of a mile of wooden shops was well alight from end to end, the flames curling upwards from horizontal timbers, and inside an orange sea of flame. Rolls of silk lay scattered on the road all the way to Capitol Corner, and at the crossroads before that, where four streets were burning together, a group of black-jacketed figures fled from the jeep's approach, dropping bundles on the road as they ran. Here the crackle of the fire became a roar and every few minutes a floor or roof collapsed in a shower of sparks with a noise like the delivery of a ton of coal. It was pleasantly warm in the burning street, and we stopped there for five minutes warming our hands at the fire.

At Capitol Corner it was only twilight again, but a roaring blaze leapt up from the bazaar by the Nai Ja apartments, and the Chosen Hotel seemed a dark island in an ocean of fire whose crackling was now the only sound in the city.

The great banner still hung between the lamp standards—you could read it in the light of the burning buildings. Someone had splashed a great 'D' in black paint at the beginning of the second word. It now read: WELCOME DUNCURK WITH BOUNDLESS GRATITUDE.

Bridge Street was blazing. The dead old man sprawled over the pavement, his white clothes now orange in the glare. At Main Supply Route corner, halfway down the last half mile, the military traffic had thinned to a trickle emerging between blazing cliffs from the north road, and the British military police were on duty on the roundabouts. The fires in North Road were fifty or sixty yards away from them, so they had heaped up a great bonfire of wood in the centre of the roundabout to keep them warm.

There were three of the Redcaps, and you could tell by their friendly and paternal manner that they were enjoying themselves as figures in this romantic figure set. The snow, the orange flames, the empty, blazing, crackling canyons of the city streets appealed to their imagination. It was a story that would last them a lifetime. Ten years ahead, maybe, on some new depressing battleground, some young soldier would talk of fires.

"Nay, you don't call that a fire, lad," some older man would say. "Ask Joe, if you want to know about fires. He was in the fall of Seoul, was Joe," and Joe would tell them, very quietly, about his night on the roundabout on the North Road.

Something of this happy anticipation showed in the policemen's bearing.

"Park up that road, please, on the right and face south," said the one who leaned into our jeep.

"Well, what do you know?" I asked him, standing on the roundabout, warming my behind at the enormous bonfire while Page went off with his camera to photograph the occasional truck or tank passing between the blazing housefronts.

"All the American traffic is through, I think," the policeman said, "or nearly all of it. Most of our stuff has gone through too. It's mostly the Royal Ulster Rifles we're waiting for now. Something seems to have happened to them, sir. There's an officer of 29 Brigade down by the river counting them in; you'll see him at the end of the tunnel when you go to cross. Oh, and we've had orders to hold up all refugees trying to cross the ice before first light in the morning."

It was a reasonable order. A whole Chinese army could have crossed as refugees. "We don't know who they are, these refugees," said the policeman, "we're letting refugee motor traffic through, of course, because we're going to blow the bridge tomorrow morning."

Trucks were passing at the rate of about two a minute while we stood there; faces under British berets peering out from between the back curtains, some in a kind of happy wonder at the sight of the burning city, some too far worn out with action and cold to wonder at all. But there was a drowsy sort of contentment written on most of them—to be moving, to be in trucks with curtains to keep the wind off, to have left action and the monotonous life of the foxholes behind for a little time; a sense of a stiff job of soldiering done, and temporarily done with: all these things wrote a kind of happiness into faces lumpy with fatigue.

As we left the policemen and moved slowly down lower Bridge street a dozen fat rats ran drunkenly across the street. The M.S.R. roundabout marked the end of the fire's progress, and twenty yards south of it the cold and darkness poured over and into us again. Ahead of us the road lay black, but seemed to run between hundreds of flickering lights at ground level, until it reached the long hump of the Han River embankment, faintly discernible as a black wall against the navy blue sky. And hardly had the crackling of the fire died behind us to a murmur when we were among the flickering lights: they were the camp fires of thousands of refugees who had been forbidden to cross the river until dawn. At the end of Bridge Street, where the policemen had stopped them, they had sat down. Moved off the road, they had claimed the pavements, and now upwards of 2,000 of them squatted there on each side of the road, two long quarter-miles of packed, enduring humanity. They had broken up flimsy houses on either side of this end of Bridge Street and were burning the pieces so as to keep alive during the night. I shall never be able to think of 'the family circle' as an abstract idea again. Here was the original primitive organisation itself. Each family of refugees had dropped its bundles and piled them in a circle, perhaps eight or nine feet across. This kept the wind from their backs as they crouched in a ring round the fire which dug a little tent of light above them out of the bitter night. A thousand of these little tents reared themselves out of the darkness as far as the base of the Han River embankment. The refugees squatted there, knees to chin, gazing into the fire, waiting for sunrise. Only the children showed the slightest animation. There seemed to be very few youths or grown-up girls among the refugees here: the most usual family group was an old man and woman with two or three children. They fed their fires with cupboards, window frames, boxes and ornamental carvings from the middle-class houses of Bridge Street. Brass pots full of rice were bubbling on some of the fires.

Bridge Street ends at the river embankment, where a square-cut tunnel of concrete, only twenty feet wide, pierces the bank and leads out to a slope of sand, the river, the pontoon bridge and the sand flats. The tunnel is about twenty yards long. At its further end and to one side a fire of logs blazed in a big oil drum, and a British officer stood there with a notebook in his hand. Beyond him the ground fell abruptly away and the road descended as a track in a series of hairpin bends to the pontoon bridge 400 yards away across the sand. The bridge was visible only as a straight line of lights moving slowly forward—the dwindling tail of the military traffic, the last of the bug-out. So far below us, the moving column looked tiny and remote, dwarfed by the immense sky which now for the first time became visible, and by the sweep and triumph of the wind, for there is no shelter on the river flats. And it was here that the real cold began. We pulled the jeep on to sand at the side of the track a few yards beyond the tunnel, and switched it off.

I think I have a neurosis about the sand flats of the Han River. When I first saw the place I feared it, and when I think of it now I still do. Of all the places in the world, it is the most dismaying; and to me it is not quite of this world. If I were set down in the middle of it alone, now, I should begin very soon to run. Geographically it is simple enough.

The embankment, which is the southern confine of Seoul City, rears itself up from a steep, wide slope of sand which falls down to the river. This sand belt is about 400 yards wide; then there is the river, 200 yards of olive-green ice; then there is a flat island of sand a mile wide; and then another arm of the river embracing this island; and then another half-mile of sand flats and a short climb to the Yongdungpo road. The whole area, and it is several miles long, is in the shape of a shallow dish, and thirty or forty feet below the real level of the land. It is arranged so that the north-west wind from Siberia has untrammelled access to every inch of it.

The ancient Scandinavians saw hell as a cold, foggy place with no boundaries. The flats are rarely foggy, but the horizon in winter is always close and blurred with wind-blown sand and ice crystals. The sand is a very pale yellow-grey dust with a half-inch coating of ice grains.

We could see none of this, of course, as we sat in the dark, but we could feel it all. The quality of the cold had changed: it was so cold that it made you afraid, and I could hear myself giving that little laugh between pain and astonishment—the one wrung from people who have knocked their funny bones or caught their fingernails in the door. It was as cold as that. We got out of the jeep and walked back to the fire in the oil drum and the British officer, who turned out to be Captain Ellery.

"Hello, Bill," I said, "what's happening?"

"Well, I make us short of more than 220 of the Royal Ulster Rifles so far," he said, pulling at his ginger moustache in a worried way.

"The Cooper Force people?" I said.

"Yes," said Ellery, and he began to give me the outlines of the action which had developed that evening in what has since been called 'Happy Valley,' heaven knows why. I filled in the gaps in this story later from men who had fought there, and now know very much more fully what was happening twelve miles north of me as I stood freezing by the great fire on the Han River bank that night talking to Bill Ellery.

It must have been about half past one in the morning then, so the action was over, and the last of the Irish prisoners were at that time being hurried northwards across the hills in the frost. But all the time we had sat 'trancebound' in Prince Li's house a horrifying drama had been working itself out a few miles up the road. Cooper Force had been a mixed force of tanks and infantry, a sort of very large battle patrol, and at dusk, headed for home, it found itself in a long, narrow valley whose steep sides sheered abruptly down on to the narrow track. It could hardly have found itself in any very different kind of country, for nine-tenths of Korea has the same sort of con-formation—steep ridges with shark-tooth peaks and narrow valleys between them. It's a bad country for tanks. The tanks were in front. Darkness fell. "You couldn't see a damn thing through the tank slit," said a tank commander, "or even if you stood in the turret. We had men on foot showing us the way." Quite suddenly, they were aware of the ambush. The hillsides were swarming with Chinese soldiers. Then the leading tank stuck and the way was blocked.

It was the Brigade's first real encounter with the Chinese mass assault—the method which the Chinese themselves called 'the human sea wave,' the mass infiltration, the ambush, the small force drowned in enemy.

"It was very queer and eerie," a soldier told me afterwards. "They came down the sides of the gully like a football crowd, and some of them were laughing. They laid hold of our legs as we sat on the tanks—you couldn't keep them off, there were too many. They didn't seem to want to kill us when they got close up, but they always tried to kill the officers. They dragged drivers out of their trucks by their arms and just took them away, laughing. We must have killed hundreds and hundreds. There was a sergeant on one tank who finished up all the ammunition in his Sten at about two yards range, and then he was knocking them off the tank with the butt end of it."

Much later, long after the stories had been told, the Rifles went back to that valley and were able to reconstruct to some extent the picture of events that night—the lone fight here and there in the blackness of this or that officer, found dead in the middle of a ring of Chinese. They could follow in daylight the strange fortunes of the little groups who escaped, slinking up gullies and climbing among the bitter ridges, hiding in little freezing parties with sentries out.

Only the barest outline of all this was known, though, as Ellery and I stood watching the trucks pass. Every now and then Ellery would stop a truck, note its number in his book and count the men inside. "How many have you got in there, sergeant?" he said on one of these occasions as the N.C.O. put his face out through the curtains at the back of the truck. "Seven, sir."

"Are they all right?"

"Are yez all right back there?" roared the sergeant into the truck.

Seoul : January 3rd—4th, 1951 (*Television Newsreel taken by Cyril Page*)

" Capitol Corner," Seoul (*Planet News*)

Seoul after the Fire (*Planet News*)

"Yes, yes," came a murmur of sleepy voices.

"Are any of them wounded?"

"Are any of yez wounded?" bellowed the sergeant.

"Three, sir," he reported after investigation.

"Well," said Ellery, "how badly?" He craned his neck into the black interior of the truck. "Are they bleeding or anything?"

"Are yez bleedin' back there?"

A weary laugh went up inside the truck.

"One, sir, but he has a bandage."

The truck rolled on and Ellery noted the figures. A little group of British and American soldiers which had formed around the oil-drum fire, chaffed each other and shivered. The wind moaned down the tunnel.

I suppose it was about three in the morning when we said good night to Captain Ellery, mounted the jeep and began to move down to the Han River bridge.

It was a bad time to make the move: jammed across the first of the hairpin bends was a vast machine bristling with cranes and rollers of cable—probably some kind of recovery vehicle— which had seen the impossible bend too late and slewed itself into the sand. Its crew and some American policemen worked like fiends at it, screaming curses into the empty black bowl of wind around them. It took twenty minutes to get it off the track, and tears of cold were rolling down the faces of its crew. The column moved on ten paces, and now our jeep overhung the slope to the river. We could see in the headlights of the column and the torches held by the policemen on the bridge the cause of this new hold-up. It was one of those gigantic motor tricycles with six seats behind the driver's saddle. Ancient vehicles of Japanese make, they had been dug out of all the old dumps up and down the country by the wretched Koreans and made to carry one more load south in their old age. This one had broken down halfway across the bridge. On the little stage, defined by headlights and policemen's lamps, the unfortunate Korean driver was giving an impassioned performance—now working in frenzied time at the kick starter, now walking rapidly to and fro, now spreading his hands and bowing in little jerks of apology all around him. From our perch on the bank it looked like one of Charlie Chaplin's early films seen through the wrong end of a telescope. Insane curses from the freezing column were flung into the wind towards him in a howl of hate.

Finally they all got off the thing and pushed it across. I could hear myself snarling with everybody else, "Oh, get on, get on, get on."

Our turn next. We were on the bridge. The naked lights slung from a pole in the sand showed a yard or two of olive-green ice beyond the rubber pontoon. Ice and pontoons were all one mass and the bridge did not give an inch to the weight of the heaviest vehicle. 'Ker-donk, ker-donk' went our jeep on the joints of the runway. We mounted the ten-foot slope at the end and we were on sand again. We were south of the river. We ran on for a hundred yards, turned off the track and stopped. I had known it with dread all the time, but hadn't dared realise it before. Without blankets, sleeping bag or whisky, I was going to spend the night on the Han River sand flats.

It was Page's jeep. Page wanted the picture of the blowing of the bridge. If Page had been stark naked he would have stayed for the picture. The prospect of the night ahead of me would not deter him for an instant. All the same, he now made a noble gesture. He held out his blanket and said: "I can let you have this, I've got my sleeping bag."

CHAPTER XII

I took the blanket, and wandered off in the d_____
small fire I could see in the distance. It turned ou_____ ___ _ery
small one—one miserable tree branch smouldering in half a
dozen places—and there was a figure lying beside it, wrapped
in a sleeping bag and packed around with blankets. I said,
"Mind if I join you?" "You're welcome," said the voice in
British, not American, and it added that the night was "muckin'
parky."

"It's twenty minutes to four," went on the figure, "and I go
on duty at four. Military police. This fire'll just about last me
out. Cor, is that all you've got, mate, one muckin' blanket?
You'll be a muckin' brass monkey by morning." I couldn't
have agreed more.

I lay down on the sand and rolled myself up in the blanket. I
was immediately frozen from the thighs to the toes and from
the neck upwards, so I unrolled myself again and draped the
blanket double around my legs. Better. My hands were frozen
now, so I shoved them down inside my parka, but I had to take
them out again almost immediately to adjust the string of my
parka hood and save my ears from frostbite. By the time I'd
done that my back was frozen, so I wheeled into a new position,
vis-a-vis the wind, and began all over again. Only perpetual
motion of this sort, I soon found out, gave you the slightest
confidence in your survival, and that only for a second or two
at a time. I had been doing it for twenty minutes and was numb
to my innermost lights, when my companion got up and said,
"Well, be seeing you, mate; I'd leave you my kit, but I'm off
to Suwon. Cor, they can have this country," and I was alone.

The next twenty minutes were the most appalling I have ever
spent. I twisted and looped like a wounded caterpillar. Great
tears rolled down my face. My parka string worked loose and

urnt agonisingly, and then stopped burning, and that angerous. But my hands were too cold to grasp the parka od string. I got up and walked about, stumbling in the pitch dark, hoping for something impossible, such as to light by accident on some wood. There was nothing but sand and the moaning wind. When I got back to the fire again it was almost out and a figure was bending over it. The fire gave just light enough to show that he was gigantic, and a Negro.

"Hey, boss," the Negro whispered hoarsely, rolling his eyes, "are you police?"

"Yo," I said. I couldn't speak properly, my mouth was too numb.

He came closer to look at me. "Well, if you're not police," he went on, "I got sumpin' here, but you gotta say you picked it up somewhere." He disappeared into the darkness and came back rolling something along the ground. "It's a drum of gasoline," he said in a bass rumble, and poured about three gallons of it over my fire.

Oh, the brave sight! The wonderful thing! The Negro and I lay down on opposite sides of four feet of flame and worshipped it.

First we held out our hands, whose presence we were aware of by their weight alone, and after a few minutes there they were again on the ends of our wrists, with fingers and everything. Then we could adjust the strings of our parka hoods and keep the cold from our ears.

At that point we became human again and able to fight against the cold. We poured the petrol until we had extended the fire to a length of five feet stretching from our chests to our feet. We had automatically taken up positions so that the tops and backs of our hoods were presented to the wind. We became so confident and clever that we even discussed the possibility of a drip feed for the fire, but ruled against it because in the unlikely event of our going to sleep we might perish in the flame. "And I dunno how long the gasoline will last," said the Negro.

We measured the length of time the last dollop had taken to die down and decided we would have to be more sparing with it.

The panic went out of us. It was now no more than terribly cold. As the green gaberdine browned in the heat in front, our backs froze and quivered with a separate life. It was still too cold and painful to talk for pleasure. I wrapped the blanket over my back and under me, and decided to try to lie still and forget my back altogether. The Negro had two blankets, which he arranged and rearranged for some time, and then apparently came to the same decision: he lay still, and I could hear at every third or fourth breath the little grunt of a man in pain or effort, and at every third grunt the Negro said,' 'Jesus''—as a plain statement of fact.

I don't know what I sounded like.

I didn't know then, but my companion must have been a driver in Captain Wagner's famous Negro Trucking Company. I don't suppose that outfit will ever get a mention from the military historians, but it deserves a very special one, because at that time in the war the ties which bound the United Nations together were at their most frayed, and the British and the Americans glared at each other when they met with suspicion and dislike, and not all the public jovialities of generals, the punctiliousness of officers, nor even the restraints obviously put upon themselves in conversation by the more responsible soldiers in both armies, could disguise an ugly atmosphere. The reason was, whatever the rights and wrongs of the affair may have been, that it was believed by several units, including the British and the Turks, that certain very sticky positions they had found themselves in during the course of the retreat had been due to a series of precipitate and unannounced withdrawals on their flanks. The sensitive Americans reacted very strongly to this belief. It was then, at the peak of this period of mutual dislike, that 'Wag's Company' was put under direct command of British 29 Brigade, and immediately an island of genuine international warmth, friendliness and esteem was created: immediately, because the Company's very first job was to bring the Royal Ulster Rifles out of their battle that night, on January 3, the night of the burning of Seoul, and take it back to base. Military reputations—among soldiers, I mean— are based on snap judgments, on hundreds of tiny pointers towards character. A split second hesitation, a small lassitude at the wrong time may be damning to the reputation of man or unit. And soldiers are practically always right in these matters.

What 'Wag's Company' did on that occasion which so endeared them to Brigade is simply told. They went further forward and stayed there longer than anybody had a right to expect of them. The Brigade never forgot it. From then until, in their wisdom, the authorities sent the Company to another front, 'Wag's Truckers' were as much part of the Brigade as any of its other units. It wasn't simply that senior officers pronounced their performance first-class; they got a higher rating than that, perhaps the only real military award: "What, Captain Wagner and his lads? Bloody all right, mate, they was."

The personality of the Company Commander had a good deal to do with it. This unconscious missionary, Captain Wagner, was a strange figure. Had General Goering had a happy youth, avoided neurosis and reached the age of twenty-eight unscarred by tragedy, he might have looked like Wag, who was seven feet high, as broad as three ordinary men and as fat as four or five. When he laughed, the doors and windows rattled, two great red apple cheeks came up to blot out a pair of guileless, circular blue eyes, and his great belly bounced up and down. He could drink two bottles of Scotch and remain on his feet in good temper. His orders, which quite often consisted of the jerk of a thumb, were obeyed with a lightning reaction which would have done credit to the Guards, but his Company spoke of him with warm sentimentality.

It was a member of his unit who lay opposite me now, saying "Jesus" at short intervals. If I'd known that I could have had a new angle on the Happy Valley story in time to make it news.

But I didn't know that, and in any case it was too cold for speech, even for reflection. I just lay there and felt, with curses and occasional tears, how cold it was. I never thought of anybody else but my suffering self that night, but I will do so now, since I am warm enough.

At that time, then, nearly half past four in the morning, twenty miles to the north of me, the Royal Ulster Rifles prisoners, half dead with fatigue, many of them wounded and frost-bitten, were marching north over the tough hills in this same deadly cold, desperately tagging on to their Chinese escorts if possible, since their fate among the North Koreans would range between the narrow probabilities of being shot or burnt alive. True, they had some prospect of being burnt alive in any case, since the United Nations air forces might well be out with napalm bombs. They went stumbling on, very hungry.

The old Korean woman on the running plate of the engine which had been in Seoul Station was enduring her ninth hour of this atmosphere. True, she was getting some heat from the boiler, but she was also resisting a thirty-mile-an-hour slip-stream. I doubt if she was dead yet. She was a very determined old woman. By then, though, seventy passengers had already perished by being swept off the coach tops in the first tunnel beyond Yongdungpo. The train didn't stop.

In Langham Place they were just finishing Radio News Reel, with no despatch from Cutforth, who had not uttered for three days.

About this time five women on the road to Suwon reached the point of insanity. They were crossing a stream where the ice was broken, so they took the babies off their backs and held them in the water until they were dead. Then they trudged on, flip-flop, flip-flop, through dust as fine as flour and colder than the water. One of the women was a Christian, and she began to sing 'Rock of Ages.' She was found wandering insane next morning, still singing it, and she sang it until she died three weeks later.

A peasant called An Kay Moon, whom I met later, was sitting in his house on the northern bank of the Han River estuary thirty miles to the north-east of us. He was sitting there with his family and his household goods packed around him, trembling at every sound, because last time the Communists came to his village the local fellow-travellers had called in and beaten him up at midnight. Now the Communists were there again, only five miles away. His belongings were packed in bundles and on an 'A' frame, and stacked against the walls of his single-room hut. He and his family were to walk south just before first light.

III

The Number One Boy in the train was asleep and smiling, with contributions from everybody else's bedding piled around and over him to keep the slightest draught from his august form.

The guns, the 105's and 155's which were half a mile behind us on the sand flats, now opened up. The big ones sent a noise like an express train roaring across the sky.

"Get on, get on," I said weakly and stupidly to myself, for I was anxious for the dawn.

CHAPTER XIII

I

THE Negro and I must have fallen asleep, if so sweet a word can be used of our mode of losing consciousness. When I next opened my eyes it was light, early light. The sky was a shadowed blue still.

I moved my head an inch and burned my mouth on a jagged mass of ice which clung to the pile lining of my parka hood where I'd been breathing, and I found to my astonishment that that was all the movement I could make without excruciating muscular pain. I was 'frozen.' This was what used to happen to the men in the foxholes and I'd heard many a lurid description of it. Everything they had said was right.

I was breathless and sweating with pain by the time I'd struggled into a sitting position, perhaps a quarter of an hour later. The fire was out and the cause of half my paralysis was apparent immediately when I sat up; my gigantic companion had moved across in the night and his head and his great shoulders were using my stomach as a pillow. I woke him up and he began to groan.

There was a litter of military vehicles on the sand flats. The old Japanese motor tricycle lay nearer the river, tilted on its side, and there were no signs of its occupants. The column of refugees had already resumed its march over the ice, though the sky had not yet entirely shaken off the night. Their file wound slowly over the flats a quarter of a mile downstream. Slowly, in pain, the Negro and I contrived to pour out more petrol on the sand and light it. I fancied I could feel my liver and kidneys as solid bodies in my inside. My ankles wouldn't work at all yet and I had to straddle about on the sand. Straddling, I moved across to the jeep and fetched an old tin, a pint of water and some coffee. There was no milk and no sugar. Page was lying asleep in the jeep, wrapped up in his sleeping bag, and I managed not to wake him up. When I got back to the fire, the Negro had some boards which he had wrenched from a wooden hut. We could now see a few hundred yards away. "There are about seventy people sleeping in there, boss," he chuckled, "and I took their house down around their ears without awakening any of them."

We made the coffee and thawed out, and by the time we had drunk it there was a twinkling of other small fires about the sand flats, and the world was awake.

It was while I was putting on another pot of coffee that I noticed, quite close to us, the most splendid and luxurious Packard motor car. It lay there among the ugly military vehicles, glittering and shining like some great lady in reduced circumstances. From its interior now emerged a small figure, lizard-like about the face under the pointed cap and dressed in a fur-lined overcoat. It was my acquaintance at the station the night before, the Old Person from Oxford, and inside the car, stretched out at ease on the caressing upholstery, were his wife and daughter and that incredible old lady, his mother.

"Ah, my dear friend," called out the Old Person, waddling across the sand towards me in the friendliest and most engaging way, "my plans en-en-en-en, as you see, have matured."

"Where on earth did you get it?" I asked.

"I paid a quite inconceivable number of won for it. En-en-en-en-en. So many, in fact, that its owner, en-en-en-en-en found it judicious to accept my very first offer and proceed, himself, on foot. I wondered at the time at this, and now it appears it was a en-en-en-en-en swindle. He was a en-en-en-en-en swindler. Some vital part of the machinery is *broken*, my dear fellow. It has en-en-en-en-en 'packed up.'"

The quotes he put around the last expression were as audible as explosions.

"What's the matter with it?"

"No man of my generation is a mechanic," the Old Person said sadly, shaking his head. "Some vital part. It will only run downhill. They had to push me over the bridge—with curses," and he suddenly hid his face behind the sleeve of his coat and tittered.

"At least," he continued, "I am across the river. 'One more river to cross.' How I *wish* that were true! There are, I believe, about twenty-three rivers between here en-en-en-en-en and Pusan."

I gave him some coffee and a cigarette. "Thank you, thank you. But I must make some return. I have en-en-en-en-en sugar. Plenty of it," and he produced a small sackful from the boot of his car and began to wrap up about a pound of it for us in an old copy of the *Stars and Stripes.*

His vitality was inexhaustible. In less than an hour he had half a dozen American mechanics nosing into the bonnet of his car.

The morning motor-starting chore was beginning, and starters churned and hammered. Vehicles began to clatter around in circles on the sand, towing refractory comrades, while the screaming and the cursing floated impotently about in the wind which was whipping the close horizon into a mist of dust and ice. The sun shone in a fleckless sky. I felt as though I'd been beaten all over, and was too tired to stand, so I went and sat in the jeep for a bit, but that was too cold, and I wept for a minute or two, thinking of the terrible effort needed to drive the jeep to the fire. Finally I did that, not just to the fire, but over it, so it licked at the running boards and I could burn my boots in it. Page by this time had gone off with his camera to film the refugees.

The refugees were massing in panic on the far bank of the river and the single file across the ice and sand had become several converging columns, each six or seven deep. When my feet were warmer I walked to the edge of the Han and watched the scene.

The cold of the night had left a white sprinkling of ice crystals like a sifting of sugar on the dark green ice of the river. On the far bank, Seoul towered up above the embankment in tip-tilted terraces. There were ice crystals glittering on them too, and all along the embankment down river from the pontoon bridge, a gaily coloured multitude swarmed along the edge of the ice. They crossed it in families, the women staggering on the slippery ice, losing their bundles, falling down, peering wildly around for the children whose hands had been snatched from theirs in some skid or fall. Some families pushed handcarts of household belongings and half a dozen bullocks had been urged out on the ice. Two of them lay where they had fallen near my side of the river, with their legs broken, bellowing dismally. The peasant who stood over them rained shattering kick after kick into their ribs. A little girl, lost, stood on the ice five yards out of the column, a small bundle on her head, her hands clasped across her ribs, and gave scream after scream of terror, but the column shuffled on past her in silence. And then the dreadful sounds of the bullocks and the little girl faded into insignificance as a great brazen voice began urgently to speak from the sky. It was the loudspeaker aeroplane, used for propaganda over enemy territory, and it had been brought up to try to persuade the refugees to stay where they were, to stay in Seoul and not to cross the river; for, not far south of the city now, the roads were impassable for the press of people. Military traffic was at a standstill and the refugees swarmed, silent and heedless, under the wheels of trucks and poured in torrents down the M.S.R. All the regulations restricting their movements to byways and railway tracks had proved useless. The railway tracks themselves were moving rivers of refugees, and the people died in hundreds under the wheels of trains.

'Stop it somehow' had been the order from army headquarters, so now the aeroplane wheeled over the river seeming to blacken the sky with the hideous scraping of its great ugly voice. It blackened it in vain. The column never even wavered. All that happened was that thousands of refugees on the further bank, who had been in no immediate hurry to leave, now scrambled on to the ice as fast as their fear of its breaking would allow them. And when after twenty minutes, the aeroplane gave up, the situation was worse than before and you could feel the hatred that followed the thing as it wheeled away south to Suwon. The next move was up to the military police.

And very soon, while everyone was still enjoying the physical relief of the aeroplane's departure, four of the police climbed gingerly out on the ice in front of the nearest column, holding their automatic guns at the ready in front of them. The face of the youthful policeman nearest to me was a mask of distress; his conception of his rôle as liberator had included no such duty as he was now called upon to perform. First, they shot the bullocks, and that act was overdue; then they moved into the column and slowly advanced, step by step, their guns pointing at the terrified people in front of them. These finally wavered and went back, wondering, step by step. And step by step, the policemen herded them, walking backwards, towards Seoul. The crowd had taken twenty steps backwards before they realised what was required of them, and then a great wail broke out from the head of the column. Women acted frenzied appeals in dumb show, men shouted, gesticulating, children began to scream. The policeman nearest me halted for a second or two and wiped his face with his handkerchief, then he pressed on slowly, inexorably, and suddenly the people turned their backs on him and, in utter woe, began to shuffle back across the ice the way they had come.

Frightful tragedies were born in that moment. A woman, surrounded by children, who stood on the bank near me, began suddenly to scream and hold out her hands towards the retreating column. She turned to us on the bank and so vividly acted her story that we understood it at once—the father of the family had convoyed his wife and children across the ice, carrying the heavy luggage, and, only a few minutes ago, had returned across the ice for another load.

We were a useless lot. An American sergeant among the group spoke for us all. First he looked around at each of us in the group, avid for signs of action. Someone should do something, but who and what? Then he clicked his tongue for about a minute and then, "I dunno," he said, "I just dunno," and he turned away. That's what we all did. The woman went on screaming among her children until she suddenly jerked sideways and began to vomit. That was something to be glad about, when the noise stopped.

When the police came back, mortars behind us lobbed their shells on to the river and broke up the ice. That was that.

The Old Person was hovering about the jeep when I got back to it.

"You are not, by any chance, driving towards Kimpo?" he asked.

It was an idea. Why not watch them burning the airstrip installation? It would be news. The gossip now was that the field engineers would not blow the bridge until one o'clock— three and a half hours away. Get away from the Han River flats for a bit, damn them.

"Yes," I said, "I might do that."

"Then if you would be so very good as to put me down somewhere on the Kimpo road . . .?"

"Certainly."

"I have another plan."

"Good," I said vaguely. I felt inexpressibly weary and dreary. The guns on the flats had begun to fire again, and were firing like mad as if they'd suddenly seen something: and they might have done, there was a spotter plane observing for them.

2

So we climbed into the jeep and drove out of the Han River basin on to the Kimpo road and past the Suwon crossroads, where an inextricable huddle of military vehicles were locked in a traffic jam which had been there since dawn. Men were asleep at the wheels of their vehicles. Trickles of agricultural refugees with carts and oxen were wandering in from the west to join the muddle on the Suwon road, and the Old Person studied these groups intently and finally made me put him down opposite one of them.

"A friend in need, I think."

"Well, goodbye," I said, "I hope we meet again."

He assured me that we should and his thanks went on for several minutes. When I drove on he was walking resolutely towards the group of yokels, exuding confidence, his head high and on his face the smile of a genial host.

A pillar of black smoke hung over Kimpo and the wooden store buildings at the entrance to the airstrip were blazing away merrily. I warmed myself at them until I was possessed by a strong desire for sleep, but I dared not sleep, of course, in case I didn't wake up in time for the next event—particularly if that should chance to be the arrival of the Chinese army. I dozed a bit. Then I went on to the airstrip and found a couple of American N.C.O.s fiddling with some piece of apparatus which ended in a hose pipe. They explained to me the marvels of this machine, which was to blow the installation sky high, and they pointed out the drums of napalm—solidified petrol—rolled up against the walls of the buildings, but I couldn't bother with it all. They were technical Americans. Among the technical British you can at least doze while the boredom they distil rolls over you in clouds, but technical Americans bring up special sacntions to prevent this. Their manner lets you know from the start that you are the privileged participant in a religious service, and that it's rude to snore in church.

I drove up and down the Kimpo road for some time watching the refugees, and wishing I could speak Korean. There seemed to be nothing else to do, so I went back to the river.

By this time there were no more than about two dozen vehicles left on the Han River flats, and these, except for the Old Person's Packard and two or three photographers' jeeps, were concerned with the bridge-blowing operation. A Company of South Koreans was resting on the part of the flats where I had spent the night. They had no vehicles with them and looked tired, I thought, but game. Once again I was struck by that peculiar jaunty competence in their demeanour—a sinister sort of certitude about everything in general which I associate with totalitarian youth organisations, the confidence of youth directed down one channel until it's a little barmy.

The artillery had packed up and left, and now at one o'clock there was a prolonged outburst of automatic fire from the south-west side of Seoul City. At least half a dozen weapons were in action, some at recognisably greater distances than others, and the action, if it was an action, continued for twenty minutes, so I sought the senior officer of the American engineering party.

"No," he said, "the aeroplanes tell us that the Chinese arrived on the edge of the northern perimeter of the city about ten minutes ago, and that was only a small advance party."

119

"When are you going to blow the bridge?"

"In about half an hour, I guess. Pity to blow it—it's a fine bridge. We thought we might be able to recover it, but it's immovable because of the ice. We would have to hammer all the ice off to get at the joints. Take days. So she'll have to be blown."

The firing in Seoul, which may have been a looting party, or two groups of local Communists quarreling or some more summary executions, had stopped, and now the ROKS (the South Koreans) got up from the sand and marched across the bridge to the embankment, which they climbed, and then lay on their stomachs poking their guns over the top towards the city. The dozen or so engineers moved hither and thither on the bridge putting the finishing touches to their arrangements. They were very thorough, and groans of impatience went up from the small crowd whenever they began any obviously new routine. At last, an officer came over to address us.

"In a few minutes the bridge will be blown. It will be carried about a hundred feet into the air and the pieces will all fall just about where you are standing now. My advice is to get well behind that truck," and he pointed one out about 200 yards away from the bank. "And take your vehicles with you."

I followed his advice to the letter. Page, however, preferred to remain, so far as I could see from my position, about forty yards from the bridge. We waited. The cameramen lifted their cameras, a handkerchief waved. Nothing happened. And then we realised that the handkerchief was a signal to the ROKS on the far bank, and amid stupendous groans they made their way slowly back across the bridge and joined us in the safety area.

There was a thundering crash. Black bits sailed up into the air and the ruptured pontoons sank in a swirl of water. It looked exactly like any picture you'd ever seen of anything being blown up. Then there was the patter of descending bits and pieces on the sand, and that was that. Page had two very good pictures. Not for the first time in Korea, I reflected on the curious nature of 'news.' During a not uninteresting morning there had been four supremely boring events, and these were the news items:

120

Refugees in a Railway Siding   *(Planet News)*

The Turks   *(Planet News)*

Refugees crossing the frozen Han River   *(Television Newsreel taken by Cyril Page)*

Kimpo airport had been burnt, the Han River bridge had been blown and the ROKS were the last to cross it, and the Chinese were in the northern perimeter of Seoul.

The refugee incident would have been news, but it had no chance with the censor, I reckoned, however lightly handled. He would visualise it used as enemy headlines about BRUTAL CAPITALIST POLICE, CIVILIANS FORCIBLY ENTOMBED IN BLAZING CITY and so on.

And the there was the military aspect of the matter. Were we entitled to tell the Chinese that the south-bound roads were so blocked with refugees as to need so ruthless a remedy? Probably not, certainly the censor would say not.

But for God's sake, I shouted to myself, the Chinese will have all that information in an hour or two anyway, if they want it, and as I rode out of the Han flats in the jeep, plagued once more by the vile cold of the moving air stream, I abandoned myself to a half-weeping hatred of the whole Korean set-up, of the intolerable tyrannies of cold and wind and censors and fatigue. We were passing the end of the Suwon road, and now, by God, we were stuck freezing in the back of a column of traffic which the bloody police had not been able to shift since dawn. No telephones, no transport worth the name. Go back to Japan and report it at long range from headquarters. Why stay here? The job's impossible.

And then we began to move forward and the washing-board road surface plunged with fervour into its assignment of jolting all my bones, millimetre by millimetre, out of their sockets. Hatred gave way to rage. It was a wonderfully Korean afternoon.

3

Driver Hoskyn drove our jeep and Page sat in front with him. It took us four and a half hours to cover the thirty miles to the city of Suwon.

At every halt refugees came up to the jeep and stood at a respectful distance from it, watching us. These people were nearly all old men and children. The bolder spirits, after five minutes of contemplation, would say timidly, with an interrogative intonation: "Suwon?" and indicate with a forefinger themselves and their belongings. We succumbed to a pair of children, a boy and a girl, aged about seven and eight, beautifully dressed in embroidered silk, who jumped up and down by the side of the jeep hand in hand, chanting "Suwon Suwon Suwon Suwon." When this produced no result, the pair conferred together for a while and then, while the little boy bit his thumb in the background, the little girl came forward to exert her whole charm. She did a perfect and finished little act. First she bowed in the Japanese style, then she held out her hands palms upwards in the suppliant's attitude, but quite formally: there was no 'rending of heart strings' about the gesture and her face remained merry and amused. Then she made a quite beautiful small movement of her hands, first towards herself, then towards the boy. Then she bowed again and said: "Is going jeepoo Suwon?" It was a little slow dance, quite perfect. We took them aboard, and they jigged up and down on the luggage for a while, the little boy then folded his arms and looked sternly out at the crowds of refugees. The little girl blew with her mouth for practically the whole four hours of the journey in imitation of the jeep's engine. "Is going jeepoo," turned out to be all the English they could muster between them.

We ground into Suwon as the twilight settled into night, through the North Gate, a squat tower with the usual three tip-tilted roofs, one above the other. It was just visible through the haze of golden dust kicked up into our headlights by the traffic. Confusion reined in Suwon. Half the army seemed to be there and the narrow streets were a bedlam of traffic and refugees. There was, very properly, an order to put out all lights, since nobody could ever be quite sure that the enemy would not produce an air force. A dozen big bombs on Suwon that night might have incapacitated the western flank for weeks. The police were doing their best, but plenty of vehicles still carried lights, and it was impossible to find space enough in the alleys to park all the trucks. In the main street, between the two lines of traffic, a Korean boy of about fourteen stood holding two terrified girls by the arms. He was exercising his male privileges by making to hurl them under the trucks and then at the last moment pulling them back again. Page leaned out of the jeep as we passed and gave him a ringing smack across the ear. They were pretty girls. We could see the boy for a long time staring after us open-mouthed.

4

From the low doorways in narrow streets and little squares red glints of cooking fires illuminated a yard or two of gutter and roadway. Against one such cave mouth the figure of a British soldier stood, silhouetted, and we just could make out that the cluster of trucks in that little square were British too, so we stopped. And then we all heaved ourselves round in the jeep and stared at the children. Now what?

"Suwon," I said. Without a word, they climbed to the ground and stood hand in hand while the little girl bowed. Then they both said, "Kaw mahp soom ne da" very loudly, twice, and ran dancing off down the street. We watched them until they disappeared in the dust and gloom. There was an uncomfortable silence in the jeep. "I expect they'll be all right," said Hoskyn at length. I didn't see why they should be. Nobody else was. Oh, well.

A corporal-cook was stirring a pot inside the red-lit doorway. His fire, a stone hearth at floor level, threw shadows about the room which was absolutely bare, square and white-washed. His mate, the soldier we had first seen, was peeling potatoes and whistling.

"What's this unit?" I asked. I said it in the wrong tone of voice, and the corporal-cook came to attention and gave the information crisply and impersonally. He thought I was some strange officer, and as such he was prepared to do nothing for me at all, so I hastened to correct the impression.

"I'm a correspondent," I said humbly, "and I'm looking for a telephone and some grub. You don't happen to know where I could find either of them?" I wished I had a bottle to pass over. This was just the moment for one, with the cook sore at having stood to attention for a nobody.

"You can have some grub here," said the cook, "but you won't get much. I'm cooking for twelve, and twelve have

123

arrived. I can give you a cup of tea," and he produced one. A very fine cook, a rare, a polite cook. I thanked him and stood sipping at the great steaming mugful.

"As for telephones," the cook went on, "if I was you, I'd try Signals, but don't say I sent you," he warned sharply, "because that little captain they've got there is just like a raving lunatic. Come to me just now: 'What are you doing eah,' he says (and the cook gave a spirited imitation of the captain's voice and stance), 'what on earth are you doing eah?' he says. 'This place is a Signals requisition,' he says. 'Excuse me, sir,' I said," continued the cook, in a slow, dangerous voice, " 'Excuse me, sir. Mr. Maltby is my officer, sir. I 'ave his orders to set up my kitchen in this place. If you 'ave any objections, sir, p'raps you will kindly complain to Mr. Maltby, 'oo,' I said, 'is now on the road to Taegu,' I said, 'and not expected back 'ere,' I said, 'before the day after tomorrow,' I said. Cor, he didn't half carry on," said the cook in his normal voice, "proper ravin'. So I should go off and see 'im if I was you. It's about a hundred yards down the street and first to the left and in a kind of yard inside of a big Gook house on the right. What's your paper?

"The B.B.C."

"Oh, ah?" said the cook, "d'you know Kenneth Horne?"

"No, I don't."

"Well you should try to meet him next time you're in the B.B.C. My sister's husband used to work with a chap as knew him. Proper comic he is. What's your name?"

I told him. "Well," said the cook delicately, "it surprises me you don't know Kenneth Horne."

I had been edging out into the street during this conversation and now I departed. "If you don't get no grub there, you can come back 'ere," the cook yelled after me, "but not after nine o'clock, mind."

"Thanks for the tea," I shouted.

"Signals have got a sentry outside," screamed the cook, "so mind and not get yourself shot."

The jeep was locked up in its chain, and Hoskyn and Page had disappeared. I knew Page had friends in some quarter-master's outfit, and we'd probably get a bed there, but he'd have to come back here to get his luggage out of the jeep. The cold was wicked. I made my way along the street from one fire glow to the next, towards Signals. A fine night for an air raid, I thought, looking up at the stars. I realised that I'd not eaten for a long time and my cigarettes were low.

Signals was not where the cook had said it was, so I began to buttonhole each hurrying figure in the street. They were always officers, and they always said: "'Fraid I've no idea. Just got in. Do you happen to know where the Q.M. is or B. Coy. or the Engineers or the R.A.S.C. or something?" I never did. Nobody seemed to know anything. I stumbled more or less by accident on Signals in the end.

"'Alt, 'oo goes there?"

"One correspondent."

"Advance three paces. What's the password?"

"I don't know, never heard of one."

"Well, 'oo are you?"

"B.B.C. correspondent, looking for Signals."

"Well, I suppose it's all right," said the sentry in a grumbling tone, looking at me with a flashlight, "we've got a flippin' pass-word only no one in bloody Suwon has ever heard of the mucker. 'Ave you got an Identity?"

"Yes. Here it is."

"All right, pass."

The raving lunatic captain was sitting in a bare room at a trestle table, drowned in the glare from one bulb above it. He looked tired. "Come in," he said, "sit down," and he waved me to the one ration box which was the furniture. "What can I do for you?"

"I'm the B.B.C. correspondent. My name's Cutforth. It's about three days since I've been able to get to a telephone. You will appreciate that the last three days make a big news story. The Royal Ulster Rifles' battle, for instance, is only part of it. Can you suggest any possible way of getting a message to Tokyo?" I was so tired that I had to think out these small sentences and then articulate them carefully.

"Well, of course, we're really only responsible for Signals up to the battalions. It's all American you know, down to Taegu and Japan."

125

"Don't misunderstand me," I said, "I have no right to any of your telephones for a minute. I'm trying to enlist your illegal support. If you were in my position, what would you do? You know the Signals ropes."

"I could send a signal for you to Taegu."

"Oh, fine," I said, "I'll just go away and type it and come back."

"Write it on this," said the captain, producing a little form which might have held twenty words. I looked at it.

"How much did you want to send?" he asked.

"A thousand words would do."

"Oh, good Lord, no. Good heavens! Have you any idea what the traffic is like on Signals now? Thirty words perhaps."

"Well, can I use a telephone?"

"Look, please go and see Major Gough. He's the (I've forgotten what he said he was), I really am awfully sorry. I can't take the decision. Major Gough's a good chap, and he has far less to do on his phone than I have. He's over there across the road in that house where the firelight shows."

"Thanks very much."

"Wish I could do something."

"Goodnight."

"'Night."

Major Gough wore a Scottish tam o' shanter and had a thin, competent face barred with a ferocious black moustache. I explained my mission and he laughed brutally.

"Good Christ! You've got a hope."

"But . . ."

"My dear chap, I've been trying to get a call in for four hours on my own phone."

"Couldn't you . . . ?"

"I'll tell you what, I wish you'd see Captain Smith. Great chap, Smithie. He'll fix you up, he's the (some string of letters)."

"Sorry to be a nuisance."

"Not at all, old boy. First right, second left, go on a hundred yards and sharp left again."

The cold was terrifying. The refugees swarmed down the road and their faces were glistening with tears of cold.

"'Alt, 'oo goes there?"

"One correspondent."

"Password?"

"I've no idea, I'm afraid."

"Well you can't come muckin' about 'ere without a password, mate, can you?" asked the voice of reason.

"I'm looking for Captain Smith."

"Well, this is his place. Got an Identity? Oh, well, all right this time, but I did really ought to stop you. 'Ere, the password's 'Little Apples.'"

"Little Apples?"

"Little muckin' Apples."

"Oh, thanks."

"Don't let on to Smithie," said the sentry.

Captain Smith was fat and jovial. "So you want a telephone, eh?" he said, obviously thinking the medical orderlies were the proper people for me.

"Yes. Is it possible?"

"No, frankly old boy, it isn't."

"Well, but . . ."

"Look, I wish you'd go and see Crossley. It's no more than a possibility, mark you, but I'd see Crossley if I were you. Take my advice, see Crossley."

I saw Crossley, and about three more of them. Tottering back at last through the maze of unfamiliar streets, I suddenly happened on the jeep. The cook's potato-peeling mate appeared in the cavernous doorway.

"Eh, coom 'ere," he said, "look at these foony little buggers. 'Ere's a piece of news for you."

Sitting on a ration box by the fire were the two children we had driven into Suwon. They were stuffing themselves with bully and potatoes.

"They coom driftin' in 'ere, as innocent . . ." said the cook's mate.

"This is a nice time to come back," said the cook, eyeing me sternly. "More like eleven o'clock it is than nine. The kids are 'aving your dinner."

"I might be able to drum up a bit more, though," he relented, after enjoying his moment of power.

First things first. I wasn't able to speak a word until I had started on the lovely food. All the time the cook's mate crooned over the children in a kind of maternal ecstacy.

"Nay, lass, get your grub down yer," he said, ladling out the spuds. "It's an 'orrible thing, is war. Nay, but it's terrible to think of these kids. Goo on, me lad, goo on! Wandering about in the cold and the dark. Nay, their little feet is frozen."

"Even Gooks is all right at that age," was the cook's contribution.

"If I was to chuck these poor little sods out in the cold again tonight," suddenly said the cook's mate, staring fiercely around at us all, "I'd never look my missus in the face again."

He went outside and returned with an army overcoat and three blankets, which he laid out near the fire.

"Yer can sleep there when you've done. Nay," he suddenly shouted, swinging round on the cook, and raising his hand in the gesture of a policeman halting the traffic, "say nowt. Me mind's made up."

There was a pause.

"Well, for Christ's sake," screamed the cook, "what have I done? Bellering at me like that! Have you gone barmy?"

It was settled all right.

Page came back soon after that. We were in luck, he said. His friendly quartermaster could give us beds, cigarettes and a drink. I don't remember any more that evening except the warmth and friendliness of the quartermaster's temporary mess, the hot Scotch and lemon, the packet of Players, the camp bed with so many blankets that I was warm. I really was warm. Just before I went to sleep I told Page the fate of my story. "It's a big story, and I've plenty to say, but technically it's dead now except that the others may have been held up too, but unless I can file it tomorrow it's as dead as mutton. I think Jim Hayes and Roly Herman probably managed to file the short piece through Brigade Signals before Seoul fell, and where have they gone to now?"

"They came down here last night and flew to Japan this morning, someone told me," said Page.

"That settles it, then," I said, "I shall have to go to the airport early in the morning and try for a plane to Taegu."

"O.K.," Page said, "I'll come too. Hoskyn can take the jeep down to Taegu."

K

CHAPTER XIV

SUWON airstrip is on the right of the main road south of the town. They were dismantling it, that is, taking down tents, burning huts, preparing to blow holes in the runway. The Siberian wind was dying that morning and there was a grey snow sky, and the false gaiety imparted by the bright-coloured clothes of the refugees had departed from the scene. Now, even at a distance, they looked wretched.

Two aeroplanes, which seemed to be whole and sound, stood on the tarmac, and a litter of wrecked ones formed the perimeter. We couldn't find 'Ops,' but in the end we found a brisk young American officer, who said: "Ops is dismantled. We have two planes going out, and that's the finish of the airport. They are going to Tokyo and to Pohang Dong. The Tokyo one leaves this afternoon, and the one to Pohang Dong, let's see, it's seven-thirty now—it goes in about half an hour. Both are empty and you can take your choice. I'm piloting the one to Pohang Dong."

"Where the hell is that?"

"Where d'you want to get to?"

"Taegu."

"Pohang Dong is twenty minutes' ride by air from Taegu. It's about on the same latitude as Taegu, and it's on the east coast. You're sure to get another plane from there to Taegu."

"Thanks, captain, we'll ride with you."

"Very pleased."

We gave Hoskyn his instructions. He was to go by the direct route, to keep in convoys if he could find them, not to travel late at night or early in the morning, particularly on the Green Diamond Route, where the guerillas were supposed to be very thick. He was to try to find a companion to ride with him, to go armed always, and not to linger in villages. We should expect him in three days. Had he enough petrol, ammunition, food, blankets, cigarettes?

He had everything, so we said goodbye to him, and presently he bumped away back to the town under the grey snow sky. A few grains of frozen snow like white shot were jumping on the hood of his jeep as he moved off.

I walked down to the edge of the airstrip for a last look at the refugees. They were still pretty thick, shuffling along down the road in silence. There were a few ox carts, one ancient motor cycle and—what on earth could that be? It looked like a modern motor car borne along in the crush at even less than pedestrian pace. It was indeed, it was a glittering Packard. Two yoked bullocks were towing it down the south road. At the wheel of the car sat the Old Person. He was too far away for his expression to be seen, but I could make out that he was smoking a cigar. A hefty peasant walked beside the bullocks, urging them on.

"The plane's empty, as I said," the captain told us, "and we'll be glad of company up front if you care to come along after the take-off. When we've levelled off at about 4,000, just come right in. There'll be coffee, and it's warmer in front. We reckon about ninety minutes to Pohang Dong."

It was a two-engine job, a green metal tube inside with rows of metal seats along the walls. She took off very quickly and suddenly, jumping in the air, while Page and I hung on the straps along the seats. Below us, Korea lay in a series of cruel white ridges as far as the eye could reach, with here and there an elaborate piece of iced confectionery representing a hill terraced with paddy fields. We were flying across, not along, the ridges.

Then we rose above the snow clouds and could see nothing but blue sky and glittering castles of vapour, so we went up front.

In the plastic nose of the aircraft the pilot sat relaxed in the left-hand seat, smoking. The second pilot, on the right, was handling the plane. We sat on the edges of two little spare bunks behind them, listening to their talk, trying to make out our position from the snatches of white landscape visible through holes in the clouds.

131

Now that I'd sloughed some of my fatigue and lost its merciful light-headedness, I was beginning to feel very worried about my story. All the material available from headquarters in Taegu and Tokyo would have been dead news now for days. What remained? Censorable matter and colour stories. Well, there was Radio News Reel on Sunday—the news of the week programme—perhaps they'd use it.

The second pilot was telling a story. He was the sort of cheerful, enthusiastic being bound to be sucked into the vortex of somebody else's personality. It became apparent during the flight that there were two great lights in his life—aircraft, and his senior officer, the pilot. He was careful to disguise his hero worship of the latter by referring to him always as 'this character.'

"So there we were over Kimpo with all this gasoline. They signalled us in, but this character says, 'Hell, no,' he says, 'I'm not landing this lot.' So we flew around and we flew around, and Jeez, was it cold, and presently we came over Suwon. And in we came, slowly, gently. I could see we were nowhere near the airstrip, and I suppose we were about a hundred feet up when I said, 'We got all the lights on the wrong side, sir,' I said. 'Take no notice of the lights,' says this character, 'at Suwon,' he says, 'I always sight myself in right dead over the tail of that wrecked C.47 they've got. And there it is now, we'll come in like a feather,' he says. 'There's only one miscalculation in your theory, sir,' I said, 'they moved that C.47 off the perimeter last week.' Jeez, you should have seen this character's face. His eyes were buggin' out like a tromped-on toads. We put her down the last thirty feet with a crash you could have heard at Pohang Dong, if there is such a place."

"Get on with it," said the pilot, "always using your big mouth."

"Surely," I said, "there is such a place, since we're going there."

"Well, this character maintains there is, and sure enough it's written on the map as large as life. Pohang Dong. But nobody don't ever seem to have landed there."

"It's one of those old airstrips which were in use back in July when the war was in the south," interrupted the pilot.

"But nobody don't ever seem to have been there."

"Well, they're going now."

It was a cheerful prospect, and when presently we sank through the clouds and a blue seascape rose against the plastic nose, I looked out with some interest at Pohang Dong.

It was a great orange-coloured beach stretching miles inland. The usual ring of jagged peaks surrounded it, but at a great distance. The sea was as blue as the Mediterranean and the sun was shining. We could see a tiny, narrow rectangle, greyer than the surrounding sand—it was the airstrip.

Whoom whoom, whoom whoom, we floated down, feather-like towards the end of the rectangle, and then the pilot suddenly said: "Oh, Jesus Christ!"

A moment later even I could see them—the rash of great pot-holes on the last 200 yards of the strip—and then, at about 100 miles an hour, we were among them, snaking from side to side, jolted out of our bunks, bounced in the air, hanging on for our lives to the backs of seats and any straps there happened to be. At last we stopped.

"Everybody all right?" asked the pilot. No one was hurt.

The pilot walked in silence down the gangway. At the door of the plane an officer peered up at us from the airstrip.

"Say, what are you doing here?"

"Say, what is this?"

They walked away together and we could hear " . . . little behind schedule with repairs," "Are the folks all crazy around here?" and "Got to get this strip working again; may need it."

So this was Pohang Dong—an expanse of orange sand, one aeroplane, two huts and a tent. One thing we noticed at once, "it's warm," we said. It was no colder than an English October day. We took off our parkas, walked off the airstrip and lay down in the quiet, warm sand under the sun. Page slept almost at once, and I found a stub of pencil and some bits of paper in my battledress and began to write my story. When I had finished it, I slept too.

The second pilot woke us up. "Your plane for Taegu lands here at three-thirty," he said, "and takes off at four and should be at Taegu at four-thirty. There's chow in a tent over there."

The plane landed punctually and we gathered our things together.

"Look, boys, its just terrible," said the new pilot, when he emerged from the plane, "but I gotta go up to Wonju with this before I go to Taegu."

"Where's that?"

"Oh, way up north on the central front. Gotta take off some big shot civilian and bring him back to base at Taegu. They're expecting the Chinese any minute up at Wonju."

"Oh, hell, can't you just flip us over to Taegu first? Twenty minutes. Come on."

The pilot had to point out that it was not his private aeroplane.

"My orders are to go to Wonju and then back to Taegu. I shan't be landing here again, but I'll lift you up to Wonju and back." We climbed in.

Back across the frozen ridges we sailed in the gathering dusk, sitting humped in the little freezing tube of metal, silent and full of hate, as it lurched and bucked between the peaks.

Wonju airstrip was the usual ugly dark patch between steep peaks. The wreck of an aircraft marked 'Royal Hellenic Airlines' lay at the end of the runway which it had overshot. It was colder even than at Suwon, much colder, the sky was grey, the snow was falling and the peaks echoed to the boom-boom of artillery—and pretty close too. The snow was more than six inches deep, and we walked to and fro in it around the perimeter for three solid hours waiting for this civilian. Thin shivering groups of unhappy men, putting a good face on their nerves, hung about the strip. "Has your pilot got room for any more?" they asked, and "What happened at Seoul? Chinese are very close here. Last reported only a mile away, could get in here any time." Darkness fell and still we all wandered about in the faint glow of yellow lamps and the blaze of an open-air log fire. It was a horrible place, Wonju.

We were not, it appeared, waiting only for the civilian (who was some sort of engineering expert urgently needed elsewhere), but also for a hospital plane to take off the wounded, who lay in a big tent on the perimeter. It came in at about seven o'clock with an American flight nurse, as pretty as paint, who superintended the loading. One bare electric bulb at the plane door glowered on them as their stretchers were lifted aboard. The still ones, with vacant, dark, glittering eyes—morphia cases, the restless ones who moved slightly and continuously under the blankets. The contorted ones, the green-faced, sharp-nosed, dying ones and those who looked happy to be free from conflict. They were all Americans, and all very young.

At nine o'clock, with guns going furiously, and shivering men standing practically in the fire, the pilot tapped me on the shoulder and said, "O.K., we go."

The plane was packed full.

"It's a tricky take-off," said the pilot, "and I want you all up as far to the front as you can get. If anyone wants to use the can, he can damn well want till we're over the peak. We just lift one wing over it if we're lucky, so I don't want a lot of running around in back here."

"Oh, Jesus, my feet are so cold," said a man next to me, and he was crying.

We made the peak, though we laboured a good deal. No one spoke. The bulb in the metal tube of the aeroplane gave out a sort of brown light, too dark to read by. We all sat humped, staring, and the cold seeped in and round and through us.

And so, some time before midnight, we sank into Taegu.

A jeep hurried us through the narrow streets, pitch black and full of cold. A lonely bulb glared over a pompous Victorian pillared porch, and suddenly the warmth and bright lights of the old squalid and joyful normality burst around us like a bomb. Familiar men sprawled telephoning in wooden arm-chairs, typewriters rattled, the P.I.O.'s sergeant with his friendly American grin was shaking my hand: "Glad to see you," and "So you made it." People thumped us on the back. "Ronnie Monson's in too, and Harry Gordon."

"How many for the telephone?" I asked. I was almost too tired to speak.

"There's six waiting. Only one long story."

"Who's got a drink?"

I took my pick of half a dozen bottles which were thrust out and chose Scotch. Thank heaven to sit on a seat that wasn't bucking like a bronco. There was a joyful cry from the desk: "Everybody's in now, no one missing." It was wonderful to hear the ordinary shop talk of journalists. "Say, I got a wonderful angle on the refugees." "Were you with Ronnie in the fire at Seoul? Jeez!" "Christ, was it cold in that plane!"

My turn came round at one thirty-five. At one fifty I was through to Tokyo and at two o'clock my colleague's voice, reassuring, competent, hauled me out of a half sleep, "Well, thank heaven you're all right. Have you got anything?"

"Yes. Will you take it? Dateline Taegu 2.5 a.m."

I dictated the first paragraph and then I went to sleep—only for two or three seconds, and then I heard the voice yelling: "Are you there, are you there?" I dictated about three more paragraphs and then I went to sleep again. My Tokyo colleague woke me up roaring, "Just a minute, in paragraph four, do you mean the burning city of Taegu, surely you mean Seoul?"

"Yes, correct that, yes correct that, Seoul of course," I said, and then very painfully I managed to finish the story. Seven minutes of it.

The room was empty now, except for the P.I.O. sergeant. "I've put you in with the Australians," he said. "Go along the passage to the right and up the stairs and it's the second door on the left. Somebody has taken your bedding up for you."

"Thank you very much. Good night."

I climbed the stairs. First on the left, second on the left. A rather battered looking wooden door, and written across it in bright Gothic letters, 'The Turdmongers' Arms.'

They used my story, or what the censor left of it, in the Sunday News Reel.

CHAPTER XV

TAEGU is a squalid town. Round a small hard core of undistinguished buildings in the Western manner, the wood and tile or mud and grass Korean huts and hovels huddle along the banks of the Naktong River. British Korean Base was there in a large, ugly, red-brick building, and the place was stuffed with minor H.Q.s of various units. For me, Taegu was chiefly remarkable for a placard in one of the mean streets which I thought testified to the resilience and flexibility of the Korean people in the face of the mysterious demands made upon them by the outside world: it said, THIS ONCE DIRTY CAT HOUSE NOW VERY CLEAN LAUNDRY. Inside, a dozen smiling girls slapped and rinsed and twisted the clothes, but the authorities viewed their change of heart with a cynical eye. Over the door an official army notice barked in iron-mouthed print: STRICTLY OFF LIMITS.

They gave official briefings to the journalists every morning in the deserted girls' school which was the Press billet. An immaculate young staff officer would point out on the map various places we knew not to have been in the news for days, and say, dead-pan: "Limited gains were made in this area."

"By whom?"

"I'm not free to alter the official wording of the despatch."

The Chinese were always referred to in this period of the war as 'hordes.'

"Enemy hordes overran a United Nations unit in this vicinity."

"How big was the unit?"

"Unit is all the despatch says."

"How many hordes to a regiment?"

"I am not free to change the wording of the despatch."

"What the hell is the good of these sessions?"

"I am not free to answer that question."

The name of my dormitory, 'The Turdmongers' Arms,' was a pretty fancy of the Australian correspondents, who had been much interested in a highly characteristic crisis which had lately arisen in Korea's economy in the Taegu area. Korea's rice-growing economy is built upon human excrement, and from time immemorial ox carts piled with small barrels have wandered about the streets in Taegu collecting the sewage from each household and paying the householder eighty won a barrel for it—about three-halfpence. The carters sell the manure to the farmers. These carts are not only noisome and pestilential in their right, but they're also exceedingly slow. The hygiene people had been looking upon them with alarm for months, fearing an epidemic, but it was the transport authorities in the end who, in a burst of fury at the hold-up of military traffic on the narrow roads, banished the carts from the streets by military edict. Then chaos reigned. The householders were left with all their excrement around them, and the stink of Taegu became astonishing. Moreover, the farmers were faced with bankruptcy because they were unable to prepare their rice beds, the carters were out of a job, and each small household in the city was deprived of its eighty won a week.

The edict had to be reversed, but for a week or two the Australian correspondents worked very hard trying to inform their public, as gingerly as possible, what all the row was about.

It was still freezing in Taegu, but much warmer than in the north, and one of the queer sights of the place was a bridge over the Naktong where the girls used to parade to pick up G.I.s in the evening. They were broad, moon-faced peasant girls, but half a dozen of them had made a real effort which was worth going to see. They were film fans, and they had contrived to transcribe Hollywood's culture of fifteen years ago into a get-up which made you rub your eyes with astonishment. There, before you, slinking up and down the freezing bridge road, were the film stars of 1935—short skirts, long cigarette holders, angular attitudes and all. It was a great effort, and it met the success it deserved.

Taegu railway station, a sprawling black junction, was the camping ground for something like 20,000 refugees. They lived in the waiting rooms, and on the platforms, and along the sides of the tracks. The trains killed a dozen of them every day. Families just sat there, around their fires. Sometimes they built little shelters of straw mats around these squatting places, mostly they just sat while the wind whistled along the railway lines and the snow settled on their shoulders. United Nations Civil Assistance Command was arranging for them to have a rice ration, and Korean medical orderlies moved among them from time to time, dusting them all with D.D.T., for a louse-borne epidemic such as typhus was much feared. There were hundreds of thousands of refugees packed into Taegu at that time, and though school buildings had been requisitioned and straw huts were being built, it was literally impossible for the town to absorb the crowds that came in every day by train and squatted by the tracks. This was in the days before they had opened the great settlement on Khoje Do Island.

I borrowed an official interpreter one day from the Korean Government offices, and set off to interview some North Korean refugees who had been given shelter in a school building. In the great schoolroom, 500 human beings had unrolled their mats and tatters on the floor. The air was full of human stink mixed with the acrid smoke from little bowls of burning charcoal, which were the cooking stoves of each family. To counteract the effect of the smoke, the refugees had broken most of the windows, so now the smoke swirled around in the room in gusts and an occasional icy spear of clean air drove a temporary shaft through the stink.

It was obvious at once that my interpreter had no intention of dealing honourably with me. He picked the family he wished to interview, said a few words to the man, received a reply of perhaps a dozen words, and began a long harangue. "He says, sir, that owing to brutal oppression by Communist Government, tortures and pains, he is at last forced to seek refuge in Southern Republic, where finding freedom and happy life long desired by self and family."

"He couldn't possibly have said all that."

139

"Certainly he say so."

I grabbed the arm of an intelligent looking and very odoriferous middle-aged peasant, gave him a cigarette, and said to the interpreter: "Ask this man if he is a farmer."

The interpreter spoke to him briefly and said, "Sir, he is farmer, ruined by impossible brutalities and impossible behaviour of North Korean Government. He hopes to find justice and prosperity now that he has moved from Communist domination."

"For God's sake, shut up," I said, "and ask him the name of his village."

But now the interpreter was offended, and he became monosyllabic and quite unhelpful. I could see that from him I should get patriotic speeches or nothing.

But then a queer thing happened. The farmer's wife, a broad, sleepy-looking woman in beggarly rags, who was hanging on to his arm and at the same time nursing a baby, said softly, "I speak English. I was school teacher. Then under Communists, not school teacher any more because I taught wrong things, they said. So married this man, this farmer."

And this is what the farmer had to say.

When the Communists came, he said, the land was redivided and the big farms went to the sympathisers and the Party members. Nevertheless, he was left with enough land to live on even with the tribute of thirty per cent, or so which had to be paid to the Government. But the year before, the inspectors came round to assess the crop when it was not yet half grown, and they assessed it, in the farmer's opinion, at far too high a probable yield. "All the same," he said, "I kept my mouth shut, for it was not good to complain." But the season was a bad one and the crop didn't come anywhere near the expectations either of the farmer or of the inspectors. Nevertheless, after the harvest, he was told to produce as tax the amount of the inspectors' assessment. "When I had done that," he said, "there was not enough left for my family to live on. The assessment came to more than eighty per cent of the actual crop. We discussed the situation, and since at that time the border was open it was easy to move south in the confusion, we packed our belongings and came into South Korea. Whatever happens here will be better than starvation, and I am strong and my wife is clever. We can live." I paid his wife for her interpreting and gave the farmer a packet of Camels. The official interpreter came stalking up to me at the door and said, "Interpreter 10,000 won." This was more than his week's wage, so I gave him 2,000 won, which he didn't deserve, and left him. He began to shout.

The next day Kim's train came in. It came in very slowly, hooting throatily and throwing up a shower of sparks from its wood-fed furnace. Part of the reason why the refugees elected to live in the station was their interest in finding lost friends and relations who might arrive at any time by train, and now a crowd of a thousand refugees surged around the train as it drew up to the platform. Two or three of them were killed in this way every time a train came in. The train was still covered with people, but the gaiety of the patchwork had gone. The bundles, the silk clothes, the faces and hands of all these people were a uniform dirty grey now from the smoke of the engine, and the people themselves were quite still: they didn't move at all. They didn't even make a gesture as the train came in, and when I approached them, I could see why. They were all frozen stiff.

The crowd climbed up on the engine and the trucks to un-clasp frozen fingers and support numb bodies. Against the sooty background of that station, the Koreans played the parts the twentieth century had assigned them, and staged their modern 'descent from the cross' in a hundred grotesque compositions. I saw the old lady still sitting staring, like a bad-tempered eagle, on the running plate of the engine. Men were unclasping her fingers from the rails she clung to. They carried her on to the platform and began to chafe her hands and rub the skin of her face. Soon, and quite suddenly, they stopped, looked at each other and wandered away. They left the old woman with her stove-blacked face and soiled clothes humped against the wall of the ticket office, still in a sitting position, with her hand grasping an imaginary rail. She was dead. Slowly, with gaspings and moanings, most of the rest of them thawed back to life around the twinkling camp fires in the dusk.

141

A rough computation by an American sergeant on the train put that journey's casualties at 170—mostly killed outright or left to die after being thrown from the roofs of coaches in tunnels.

Kim was there, wreathed in smiles, and I made haste to pay the Number One Boy for his good offices. The luggage was all quite safe. I settled Kim into 'The Turdmongers' Arms,' paid him enough to live comfortably in my absence and caught the plane to Tokyo for a week's rest.

CHAPTER XVI

In the Press Club, at No. 1 Shimbun Alley, double glass doors excluded Tokyo's prevailing stink of bad petrol. Two *Niseis*, girls of Japanese race but American birth, screamed into the microphones at the telephone exchange behind the desk. "Mashee mashee, annone. So desca? Hi-hi, Mr. Robinson, *Mr. Robinson*, MR. RAHBINSERN, telephone!" They were completely bi-lingual, and, I was told, the highest paid telephone operators in Tokyo.

There were rigid castes among the correspondents, and it took me some time to work out how these things were arranged. It appeared that the main body of working newspapermen whose assignment was the Korean war, and who flew into Tokyo for brief rests from time to time, were regarded as the proletarians in this society.

There was a sort of middle-class composed of correspondents resident in Japan and old Japanese hands and the chiefs of agency bureaus and any well-known correspondents. From the Tokyo fixtures the real aristocracy, the 'party members' so to speak, were drawn. They all had jobs on the committee and ministered to the requirements of the members by employing, for instance, the 'highest paid telephone operators in Tokyo,' and by choosing whose photographs should hang each week in the bar above the legend "These correspondents drank here," and by proclaiming at meetings, with the quiet triumph of those who owed it to themselves, the enormous quantities of drink 'the committee has been able to purchase' for the club cellars.

These 'party members' had devoted much time and study to the production of a special manner and gait. They moved among the crowd at a slow lope, with a good deal of arm-swinging, rather like school prefects or London policemen on duty, and held out their faces for inspection as they 'proceeded,' with such an air of noble charm that I was fooled for a bit into supposing that they were visiting politicians.

"Well, young man?" said one of these Beings to me one day, with patrician condescension.

Should I stand up?

"Who the hell's that?" I asked my neighbour when he had gone.

"The secretary."

"Of what?"

"Of the club."

"Dear me."

Modes of address were nicely graded. Brooks, for instance, as the head of Reuter's agency would get a nod and "Ah, Brooks" from the Shining Ones, but "Well, young man?" was all the proles could expect, and this insufferable mode of address was made still more curious by the fact that some members of the committee were themselves so young as to be still in the spotty stage.

I had no idea Americans ever went on like this. I thought it to have died out with Thackeray's footmen, or at latest with pre-1914 English commercial travellers, and I spent many a happy hour sitting with an 'old-fashioned' watching the big shots at their work.

They had, apparently, only two subjects of conversation. One was their familiarity of the bearers of famous names, "Knew him when he was just plain little Joe Bloggs," and the other was Mr. Randolph Churchill. Mr. Churchill, it seemed, had tried to buy himself a drink in the Press Club, though not a member, but had been detected and frustrated in this rash act by the prefects. It was a story which the proles, even in private conversation with newcomers, rated at not much more than a small paragraph; but it had lasted the committee for months. The saga of their courageous actions, high principles and noble speeches on that occasion could last several hours.

A member of the aristocracy, by right of long residence and the famous name of his newspaper, was Frank Hawley of *The Times*, but he held no office and did not feel called upon to address anybody as 'young man.' This was a great piece of good fortune for me, because Frank knew Tokyo as few people knew it. His Japanese was fluent, colloquial and scholarly. He knew everybody and he was delighted to find that I really did want to try, for instance, Japanese food and drink. He himself lived on Japanese food and knew every queer little restaurant and eating-house in the city and what its speciality was. Under his guidance I started out on a tour of gastronomic discovery which might have lasted a lifetime.

Nearly every evening, as dusk fell, Frank and I would set off along the main street called A Avenue by the military authorities: we would pass by the green moat and sloping granite facings of the Imperial Palace enclosure, past the frowning Dai' Ichi building, the seat of MacArthur's government, where the two immaculate guards with polished helmets stood all day at the entrance. We would leave A Avenue full of the stink of petrol and the clang of trams and the G.I.s parading up and down with their Japanese girl friends, and turn off past the Ginza—the chief market street, with its rows of brightly lighted stalls—and turn southwards into the Tokyo of miniature streets not much wider than a jeep. Rows of paper lanterns of all shapes and sizes hanging outside the tiny fretted doorways of little wooden houses made a sort of glowing twilight in these streets, whose main charm was the plain exquisite carpentry of each little wooden front. We would dodge under a row of tiny linen banners advertising some eating house and enter, perhaps, Mr. Osaka's *Ten Mo* restaurant, famous for its *Tempura*. In fact, it was a fried fish shop, and I can only suggest that the fried fish industry of England send a working party to the Ten Mo to investigate its methods.

The *Ten Mo* was one small, plain room in wood. It had a low semicircular bar at one end, with seats around it for the guests. The bar was of scrubbed white wood. After a tremendous bowing and hissing performance from the whole Osaka family, who owned and ran the restaurant jointly, fat Mr. Osaka, beaming like a bishop, apron and all, would mount the platform behind the bar. His wife, whose wide smile of gold teeth looked like a hand of cards, put before us the complicated assortment

L

of bowls, saucers and little raised bamboo mats which are the proper tools for eating *Tempura*. First, for each guest, there were placed on the bar two little bamboo mats like tables six inches square and about three high and covered with absorbent paper. These were placed forward of the guest and on his left and right hands. In front of these were two little bowls, a piece of china shaped like a bamboo shoot on which rested the chopsticks in their paper envelope, and a minute cup to hold the *sake*—the hot rice wine.

You began the meal with a cup of tea—milkless, sugarless, very transparent tea—in a handleless cup. Then Mrs. Osaka brought round a charming little pot like a teapot and poured out of it some soya sauce into the little bowls. You took your bamboo chopsticks out of the envelope and snapped them apart, for they were really one piece of bamboo sawn not quite through, and took up from a bowl in front of you some green grated radish and mixed it with the soya in one of the little bowls to make a piquant sauce. Then you began your *hors d'œuvres*—raw prawn. Mr. Osaka shelled the wriggling prawn and flipped it on to the left-hand bamboo table. You picked it up by the tail with your chopsticks, dipped it in the sauce you had made, ate it, and put the tail down on the little table to your right.

After a couple of raw prawns, Mrs. Osaka, coming behind you, whisked the little bowl away and you mixed a fresh bowlful of sauce, this time with white radish, more appropriate for fried fish.

Then followed a long succession of extraordinary and delicious mouthfuls—as many as twenty different kinds of fish fried in batter, and tossed, chunk after chunk, on the little table on the left of you. There was a special order to eat them in and some were to be enjoyed not so much for their flavour as for their consistency. One, particularly, was like a firm apple to bite. There were pieces of *tai*, or sea bream, octopus, eel, whiting, trout, the tough shell fish called *abalone*, and prawns. Pieces of lobster and sea centipedes. There were several different kinds of mushroom and fungus and shell-fish fried in batter. Mrs. Osaka and her daughter kept pouring the hot *sake* into the little cups, and we were formally toasting each other and the members of the Osaka family in turn while these odd and delicious titbits succeeded each other without pause. Then there was a fish soup served in a teapot whose lid made a bowl, and whose spout was stuffed with cress to flavour the soup. Then the bowl of rice—each mouthful scooped up in a dark green leaf of seaweed. Then more prawns. Then another soup, of tiny red mushrooms this time, and then, when finally the strenuous business of declining Mr. Osaka's further invitations was over, another cup of tea, brown this time, not green, and then, conventionally, a few strawberries or other soft fruit.

And then too, the first time anyway, the strange discovery that the *sake*, which had not made any more difference to your head than a similar quantity of beer would have done, had completely deprived your legs of their functions. Such is *Tempura*. I am told that the fish which populate the Japanese seas are very much the same as our English fish, but the Japanese have more than 200 species which they consider edible and almost as great a number of ways of cooking them. *Tempura* is just one way. There are also *Sushi*—shell-fish and crustaceans stuffed with rice; *Sashimi*—tenderest thin slices of raw fish with various kinds of radish as accompaniments. There are other famous meals—*Sukiyaki*—a fry of chicken or beef with vegetables and soya.

There's a wonderful restaurant, quite small and quite insignificant, where you can get nothing but the flesh and eggs of birds. *O Tori*—big bird or phœnix—is the name of it. Here they grill to a perfection I cannot begin to describe quails, chicken legs and slices of fat duck, basted and smothered with soya sauce until each piece has a surface of shining black. And there's a strange bird called a *Ban* which lives in the rice paddy fields and is very nearly spherical in shape. In the *O Tori* they turn it into a roast which, I believe, cannot be bettered anywhere on earth.

These places were 'off limits' to G.I.s, for the American authorities had a dread of bacteria which went to obsessional lengths. Any foreign food, and practically any foreign article at all not wrapped in cellophane was suspect to them, unless it was a girl.

But if the G.I. was denied the delights of Japanese food, he was denied little else. The army rioted in leg-shows, naked shows, brothel shows, dance halls and beer dives. They 'held the gorgeous East in fee' very thoroughly. Many of the Staff men were practically globular in shape. Nobody ever seemed to do any training, but there was a curious survival of the Puritan attitude. At least three fat boobs I met explained at great length, holding me with a boiled and earnest eye, that they took their Japanese girls to bed mainly in the interests of 'democracy.'

"Democracy begins among the women," roared one bitter-tongued, wise-cracking American correspondent, "out of the home and into the gutter is the policy." He was a little unfair. The Occupation had, in fact, begun to disrupt, particularly among the women, the old authoritarian Japanese system, though the new conception manifested itself chiefly, Japanese friends told me, in an almost universal, and to Japanese minds very shocking, disobedience by children of their parents in the name of 'democracy.'

This high carnival in Tokyo went gaily on until that dread day when General Ridgway came to reign in the Dai' Ichi building, and suddenly high-ranking officers were bidden to attend conferences at ungodly hours like half past eight in the morning, and a very stark notice addressed to 'OBESE PER-SONNEL' was to be seen in Service billets, and platoons of globular soldiers, with buttocks like pumpkins, rolled endlessly up and down the roads at the double, sweating and in agony.

One thing I was astonished to find in the Press Club was that only very few other journalists—notably Robert Guillain of *Le Monde*—tended to see the war, as I saw it, primarily as a story of the sufferings of the Korean people. Many newspaper-men had been instructed by their papers to play down this aspect of the matter, and, of course, some of the 'big shots' had to get an angle where their personal reminiscences of Japanese statesmen could tell the story of the Korean war.

I found it extraordinarily difficult to make up my mind to go back to Korea. I had once seen a correspondent in the Tokyo Press Club, dressed up in his padded and bulging parka, sitting crying on the sofa surrounded by his friends, because his paper had ordered him back to Korea. At the time this had seemed incredible, but now it seemed, I thought, perhaps only expressed a little too strongly. The clean sheets and early morning tea in the Marunouchi Hotel and the myriad bright little Japanese restaurants, the iced drinks and smart service of the Press Club and Frank Hawley's amusing and erudite conversation—these things seemed very dear when I thought of the black night, the freezing wind, the ruin, the desolation, the pervading fear and pain of that terrible land across the sea to the west. I put off my departure one day and was about to postpone it again when I realised abruptly that if I went on in that way I should never go back to Korea. So in that very five minutes of realisation, before my resolution had time to cool, I booked my place on the courier plane to Pusan and signalled 2 P.R.S. to send me a jeep there. I proposed to drive right up the peninsula to the front line.

CHAPTER XVII

PUSAN was the Mecca of all the refugees, and it was stuffed with them. About 300,000 had somehow managed to cram themselves into a city of half a million inhabitants. The authorities, Civil Assistance Command, were making frantic efforts to inoculate, vaccinate and delouse this great host of wanderers, for they feared an epidemic when the frost loosed its grip on the land. They had begun their colonisation schemes on Khoje Do and Cheju Do, the big islands to the south, and they had camps in and around Pusan itself. I went to one of these camps with a special mission. I was obsessed by this time with the refugee aspect of the Korean War. I wanted to find, if such a thing were possible, what the impact of the war was on the average Korean, and for this reason looked up the reference books to discover who, indeed, was the average Korean, and I got a very plain answer.

The average Korean was a rice farmer with a family of four children, and he also supported his parents. The average rice farm was just more than three acres and the average farmer was in process of paying for it over twenty years by means of the new land reform scheme which the Americans had persuaded the South Korean Government to adopt. I made enquiries and discovered that just such a man as this was to be found in one of the refugee camps outside Pusan. He had drifted down from the north of South Korea, was thirty-four years old and the average Korean in every major particular. His name was An Kay Moon. I resolved to get his story from him and accordingly set off with a team of three interpreters, because I did not care to be at the mercy of any particular point of view. I worked on An Kay Moon for four days, and this is the story he had to tell:

"My farm is about three acres, mostly of rice paddy but with a strip of ground for dry crops, and it is situated in South

Korea about twenty miles south of the Parallel not far from the northern shore of the Han River estuary. I have a wife and three children. Six years ago my father decided that the time had come for him to retire, to take his place among the village elders, to have more leisure for gossip and pipe-smoking and chess games among his friends, and to hand over to me the direction and the hardest work of the farm. All the family work on the land, including the children. We live in a small village of thirty or forty houses surrounded by high, steep hills and I am of the fourth generation of the family to farm this particular piece of land. Ours is a hard life in the sowing time, the transplanting time and the harvest time, when every member of the household works in the fields from dawn till dusk, but there are long days of leisure and festivals with dancing and music and wine drinking, and in the winter, when the ground cannot be worked, you could say we lived an easy life.

"We were working hard when the war broke out in the summer and we had no time to bother with politics. There were very few farmers who wished to leave their land and move south. Most of them said, 'What use am I without my farm?', and they said, 'Even if the Communists are devils as they say, they will still have to eat, there will still be a need for our rice.' So they stayed. It was not very different at first. Some strangers with a great many words called at my house and explained that there was now some different system in the way of holding land, and that the fraction of my crop which formerly I set aside to pay for the land under the Government scheme would still have to be paid, indeed a little more, but now, they said, I owned the land myself. It was mine. Now there were in our village some young men who had always sympathised with the Communists, and these now became very prominent in the village councils, and then it was decreed that these men, who had owned very little, should own more land. So land was given to them, and among the acres they acquired was one of mine.

"I protested against this action in the village council, where any father of a family may speak. I said that these men were full of political wind but were notoriously poor farmers; moreover, they now owned twice as much land as anyone else in the village. When I sat down there was a silence and nobody else spoke on that subject. In the next council it was objected against me that I had been a member of the Security Committee—a sort of village Home Guard for police work and to maintain order in the troubled times that had come upon us. It was only two nights after that that three of these young men came into our house at midnight, dragged out my father and myself and beat us with sticks until we nearly died. My father was ill for weeks and could only lie and groan. My family now made no appearances in the village; indeed, I was so frightened that I dared not be seen about the place at all. I wandered around the countryside calling sometimes after dark on my blood kin in other villages, and they would give me a meal and let me sleep. And often, also after dark, I visited my own family. If anyone came calling for me, my family would give out that I had gone south.

"Then came the Allied landing at Inchon, and the Communists withdrew from the village as quickly as they'd come. Shortly afterwards the police arrived to make enquiries, and I denounced to them the three young men who had beaten my father and me. The police took them away. [It is quite likely that these three wretched youths were among the group which had been shot in the trench in the Brigade B echelon area.]

"After that the land was redistributed again in the old fashion. I received my acre back and things went on in much the same way as they had always done, except that there were now a great number of aeroplanes, and for several weeks while the Communists were in our area there was danger from bullets and bombs, and particularly from the firebombs. A village not far away from ours, where the Communists stayed and billeted their troops, was completely wiped out one day. I became more frightened of these machines," said An Kay Moon, "than I had ever been of anything in the world. Another thing that happened was that the tanks drove across some of the rice paddy terraces belonging to people in the village and that upset the balance of the water levels and meant an almost certain loss of the crops unless much immediate labour was forthcoming to mend the banks. The village council decreed that all the men should give some of their time to refarming the breaches, but just as we had finished the work the tanks came again and it was decided to abandon the strips nearest to the road. There were only three casualties, all told, in our village from bullet rounds, and that was a great piece of luck. Relations of ours had terrible stories of shells that burst in their street and maimed dozens at a time, men, women and children.

"It was terrible news when we heard that the Communists were coming back. The decision whether to evacuate the village or not was left to the old men, of course, and they never came to any clear conclusion. In the end most people decided to stay. I knew it would be my death if I stayed, but somehow, partly because it was difficult to face such a change, such a loss, and partly because I was used to having the elders decide such important questions, I stayed until it was almost too late. It was on the evening that I learned that the Chinese were only seven miles away that I finally made preparations to go. It was no use starting before daylight, but when we had packed all our belongings we sat in the house, afraid, because in those days you could not trust anybody. It was true that the police had made very thorough investigations and dragged a number of people away to gaol, but nobody trusted his neighbour any more. There were plenty of people who would have liked my land, and a good way to claim it and to show their sympathies with the Communists would have been to attack me again, since I now had some notoriety as the man responsible for denouncing the three youths to the police. So when we had packed all the things we sat up all night in case of an attack. My father had decided to stay. He was too old, he said, for the roads, and so was my mother. It was decided then that my wife and I, our six-year-old son and our six-month-old daughter should make the journey, and the four-year-old daughter would stay with my parents. We dressed just before dawn. My wife put on her best silk clothes, partly because they were among the most valuable things we possessed and that was an easy way to carry them safely, and partly to show well among the folk upon the road. She carried the young child on her back and her bedding and spare clothing done up in a bundle on her head. My son also carried a bundle, and I had an A-frame on which I had packed what few saleable articles we possessed: a lacquer box from Japan, a vase I had heard people say was worth money, and also the cooking pots, a big measure of rice, my clothes and bedding and whatever else was too heavy for my wife to carry. As dawn broke we said goodbye to my parents with tears. I had never been more than six miles away from the village in my life; my wife had never been out of it.

"The Han is a sea-water estuary where it passes near my farm, and even the hardest winter does not freeze it. You can cross it by a ferry boat which plys from a village on the shore about a mile and a half from our village. It did occur to us that we might be too late, that the ferry might not be running any more, but when we began to descend the village street to the landing stage people told us that there was a boat in but that it was so full of refugees that for the last hour it had been accepting no more passengers and was due to start at any moment. When we reached the landing stage we were only one small group in a great crowd of refugees who had been refused places on the boat. When I saw that I was very frightened, for there is no other place to cross the river for twenty miles along the shore. It seemed to me that my need to go south was greater than anybody else's, since I was certain to be killed if I stayed. I told my wife what was in my mind and took up my position very near the edge of the landing stage where the plank which led on to the boat came ashore. I was desperate. I said goodbye to my wife and children in a low voice so that no one else should suspect my plan, and then when the moment of departure came and the people left on shore set up a wail, I waited until the sailor had his hand on the gang-plank to shift it away and then I ran up and clawed my way on to the boat. The sailors and the refugees who had places in the boat beat me about the head and tried to throw me in the water, and some of the men on shore tried to follow my example, but the sailors managed to throw the gang-plank in the water with the leading man on it, and when the boat left I still had a foothold. The people in the boat grew tired of beating me long before we reached the south shore. After that I walked south. I kept to the footpaths and tracks after the first four or five miles, for I had seen many people killed and injured by traffic even in that short distance. All the way to Pusan I moved in the column."

An Kay Moon said the most shocking thing about the journey, to his mind, was the way old people were shouldered off the road by the young and fit. "Many people died on the way," he said, "mostly pregnant women and very old men. There were many lost children. I helped so far as I could at three births which occurred in my part of the column on the road. The ground was too hard to bury the dead, but we moved them off the track into nooks and corners in the rice paddy. It was very hard going. I am a man in the prime of life and used to labour, so I was better off than almost anybody else in the column. I made about twenty miles a day until, after a very cold night when I had to sleep out by the side of the road, I caught this cough. [He had pleurisy.] Then I went very slowly."

"And the people in the villages you passed through," I asked him, "were they helpful?"

An Kay Moon appeared not to understand the question and the interpreter began, smiling, to say: "Sir, he finds it difficult . . ." when An began to speak again and the interpreter said:

"He says, sir, of course if you had relations in any village you could quarter yourself upon them for an unlimited period, for that is a family obligation, and this man says he had a list from his parents of all his known relatives who were living in villages on the way to Pusan."

"But the ordinary people of the villages, didn't they help?" I asked. The interpreter held a long conversation with An about this and then said: "An Kay Moon says he has heard that in some Christian villages it did not matter whether the refugee was a relation or not, he would still be given food and space, but, sir, this does not state the true case. The people in the village kept their food and space for their relatives as a family obligation and sacrifice: it would not do to give it all away to strangers and then have to tell their kin coming afterwards, 'I have given away what I owe to you.' That would be shameful. There is no question of refusing help, but the food and warmth belong to the family."

"The Government also helped," said An Kay Moon. "There were schools in several large villages where a family could stay under the roof and receive rice free of charge. The rice supply did not bother most of us. We had as much as we needed, at least for the first half of the trip. Rice is heavy—you can't carry much of it, and in the villages which the Communists were re-occupying the bottom had dropped out of the market for heavy things. The price of an ox fell to about fifteen shillings and many families ate their oxen before they moved. Rice was being given away. Anybody who had valuable, small, light articles could get fantastic prices for them. A refugee moving south would sell his oxen and all his spare rice for a watch, for instance, which he could sell on the journey."

When An had arrived in Pusan, where he had no relations to help him, he had drifted to the railway station and sat there with the others along the railway lines, nursing his pleurisy as well as he could, selling small articles for rice and firewood. That was where the Civil Assistance people picked him up. They housed him in the big straw hut, fifty feet long, in the shape of an inverted V, where six families also lived. They inoculated and vaccinated him and dusted him with D.D.T. They gave him a regular allowance of rice and even a small allowance of money—enough for him to have his shoes repaired and his hair cut and to buy a couple of pipefuls of tobacco from time to time.

What was to be his future? There was a certain rather smug feeling among the Korean officials of whom I asked this question, that, naturally, when he was in better health, he would join the army. When I asked An if this were his ambition, he looked away from me uneasily. It was almost certain that as soon as he was better he would join the other able-bodied refugees in the search for work. He would try to hire out his muscles for porter-ing or rough labour on the roads. There are practically no farm labourers in Korea, where the landless countryman is a rarity. I could see in An's eyes that he would try by any means to avoid the army. Probably in the end the authorities would send him to the refugee settlement on Khoje Do island, where he would be able to go on with the only job he knew how to do expertly—rice-growing.

And you may ask, why was not An Kay Moon in the army in any case? The answer is that there was no conscription as we know it in Korea. Not that the authorities were at all averse to coercion, but there was no regular census. The country's economy collapsed at once if the farmers were taken away, and though a rough kind of conscription effected by closing the ends of some city street and having the police pick out all the men of military age in it by guesswork was a common sight, the average countryman was left on his farm. A rice farmer's job was normally treated as a reserved occupation. That was the main reason why the farmers stayed on no matter which army occupied their territory. This time, though, they had miscalculated their position: the Chinese, when next they retreated, took with them practically the whole able-bodied population.

CHAPTER XVIII

I

Driver Robbins, whom the Public Relations Section had sent down with my jeep to Pusan, set out with me at eight o'clock one morning for the front which was now about twenty miles south of Suwon. I had been sharing a tent in the British transit camp with a genial major whose life since the fall of Pyongyang had been complicated by his adoption of two strapping young Korean women—very respectable and rather plain school teachers. The major had responded to their cries and entreaties on the roadside to the south of that city by giving them a lift to Pusan in his truck, and I think he had already begun to have his regrets. "Meet my daughters," he would say, rather wryly, for the young women had wasted no time in bringing an interpreter to explain to the major that he stood now "*in loco parentis*" and that their food and clothes and living space were now his responsibility. In return, of course, they would be dutiful daughters: they would clean his tent and sweep and dust and make the beds and pay their respects at the proper times and seasons, and let there be no nonsense. Whether he liked it or not—that was the compact.

I said good-bye to the major, and Robbins and I started along the rackety road towards our first objective—Taegu—about 130 miles to the north of us. We were stiff, bruised, weary and very cold indeed at lunch time when the mileometer showed seventy and we pulled into a compound which housed an American unit. The major in charge gave us lunch, and afterwards said to me earnestly:

"What weapons are you carrying up to Taegu?"

"Well, the driver has got a sten gun," I said, "and I have a 38 revolver and about half a dozen rounds."

"I ask you," the major said, "because the guerillas are out further up. They attacked one of our convoys about twenty miles up the road from here at dawn this morning and killed everyone in it. I don't want to make a song about it, but you must know yourself that they always tend to attack lonely jeeps. I can give you an automatic rifle, and fifty rounds and I'd feel happier if you took it along with you. Probably, though, you'll be all right if you travel in daylight and move fast through the villages."

I accepted his kind offer very readily, and then the major, with the usual hospitality of American commanders, began to inquire about my other stocks and stores. When I left him at about two o'clock I had, besides my rifle and ammunition, a big box of rations, two tins of sweets, two packs of cigarettes and about half a hundredweight of soap. We rattled on. We passed the village where the guerillas had ambushed the convoy —it was easily recognisable by the fresh bullet marks on the walls of the houses all along the street. There didn't seem to be anybody there. It was silent and empty. The next village was deserted too, and we were just pulling out of it when something went wront with the jeep; it came to a coughing halt, and then the engine expired. That was a very unpleasant half-hour I spent on sentry go round the jeep with the American's automatic rifle in the waning evening while Robbins toiled at the engine. "It's this dust gets into everything," he kept moaning. There wasn't a spark of life in that village, which was a dark, dilapidated, tragic place. The wind moaned in the nasty silence and there was nothing to see but the cold peaks ahead, the dead street behind and the lumpish jeep on which we depended for our lives. Finally, Robbins made it go and we rattled into Taegu not long after dark.

2

Kim had become boy-of-all-work and general spiv in 'The Turdmongers' Arms'. He washed and laundered and cleaned boots and jeeps and ran messages and did the shopping for a dozen correspondents regularly, and often for another dozen or so in the next room.

When all the other correspondents had clattered off down the stairs for their evening meal, I told Kim that I proposed not to take him to the front with me because he could be more useful in Taegu at the receiving end of the messages I should be sending. I told him I expected my affairs to take first place in his list of duties since I had rescued him from Seoul according to contract and was still paying him wages. He agreed, and said that this would be so, I was his father and his mother, and, just to prove his point, he put his hand in his pocket and pulled out all the money I had left him to live on during my absence in Japan.

"You have," he insisted, thrusting the mucky notes towards me, "I get plenty." He expanded a little and told me something of his new way of life.

It appeared that he had been able to convince about a dozen correspondents that he gave them personal and exclusive service, so he pocketed a dozen salaries. His emoluments from salaries alone, he told me, amounted to about £20 a month. Then there were the tips. For going down to Black Market Street and buying a bottle of whisky, an American correspondent might give him as much as 50 cents, and he cleaned their boots at 10 cents a time. Moreover, the stall holder in Black Market Street gave him a regular rake-off for his custom, and Kim had another source of income: he often asked to be paid in cigarettes or beer, or cast-off clothing: these things were worth astonishing prices in Black Market Street, and he had a valuable little side-line in pimping as well and was the agent of various 'Dance Halls' in the city.

Kim reckoned his total (and untaxed) income at the time at about £35 a month, which was a rich middle-class salary in Korea. He got his board and lodging free but had to pay a five per cent. cut on his tips and salaries to the Number One Boy, who now beamed upon him as a money spinner, almost a junior partner. I impressed upon him, once more, that the relaying of my messages would have to come first in his schemes, and gave him back his money. He told me that when he had made his fortune (which he put at about £250) he was going down to Pusan to find his mother.

'Slight gains in the centre' was the gist of the briefing in the Press billet next morning. The Chinese advance had come to a halt south of Suwon and the United Nations were fighting back. This astonished me. I wondered for a time if the communiqués and briefings were perhaps simple lies—pieces of propaganda for purposes of morale—but decided that they couldn't be. Perhaps this new general—what was his name?—Ridgway, had really been able to do something.

Robbins and I set off again on our journey north soon after ten o'clock that morning, and we were bumping along the squalid, stone-paved towpath of Taegu's canal-plus-sewer when, in a charming little yellow courtyard under a great stone image of Buddha, we saw a general sitting. Something about his face remined me—yes, I had seen it in the *Stars and Stripes* recently—it must be—it was—General Ridgway. On an impulse, I stopped the jeep and walked over to the General.

I had five minutes' conversation with General Ridgway, and when I left him I had no doubt that the United Nations were going to win the war, and win it quite quickly. I was no longer interested in this dawdling journey up to the front, I wanted to catch an aeroplane and get there at once.

The General began by telling me, very coolly and civilly, that he did not give exclusive Press interviews, and I told him that I had no intention of using what he said as news. I wanted to know what the position was: what was going to happen on the front?

"We're going to try and roll them back," the General said.

"Do you think we'll be able to do that?"

"Yes."

General Ridgway paused before each of the answers he made and seemed to calculate, or rather, seemed to bring his calculating mind to the point of speech.

"Yes," he said, "we should do that," as if he had just worked it out by algebra. He spoke in a very even, reasonable voice, musical and pleasant, but I had the feeling then and in later conferences that he was not addressing me, he was addressed

M

to the problem, whatever it might be. However pleasant and candid his smile was, his eyes were always concerned with something at the back of his mind. He had the most reassuring face. I had the strongest impression of a man who could 'remove mountains.'

Only a few days later, at a Press Conference he gave in Taegu, he outlined the whole of his plan. It was a simple plan which depended on first-class ability in his armies, and there was nothing subtle or especially ingenious about it.

"The plan is to push right through in the centre, fighting our way on foot up and down the hills in the old-fashioned style," said General Ridgway, "and get on so far that either they'll have to abandon Soeul to save their flank or we shall be able to take it in the rear. But I'm not worried about Seoul—it only has prestige value. We are out to destroy the enemy's armies, and part of the plan is to try to make it appear that we must have Seoul at any price."

Said quite straight like that, and by General Ridgway, it never even began to sound preposterous that the United Nations' armies could win a great foot-slogging offensive up the mountain spine. The word 'horde' and its connotations seemed to have faded from the military vocabulary. It was typical of the General also that he gave the Press so much information with so few heroics. He gave it all to them, and then explained in his candid voice that if this plan were known to the enemy it could have little chance of success. There wasn't a voice raised in expostulation at his conference. When he had done with us we felt as if we were winning the war too.

I left him sitting very upright under the Buddha with his kind, aloof expression and the famous grenade tied to the lapel of his uniform. He had impressed me so much that I was shaken. In five minutes I had had to abandon a whole attitude.

"We're going to win the war," I told Robbins.

"Well," he said, "it's about time."

4

From Taegu northwards there is practically nothing left of Korea. The Main Supply Route, execrable as a highway for its entire length, wanders listlessly between ridge and rice paddy through a litter of rusting T34 tanks, smashed trucks, old telegraph lines, telegraph poles askew like a row of bad teeth, wretched villages all ruined and desolate tracts of mauve-coloured ashes which once were towns. On the sharper bends of the roads in mountainous country all the paraphernalia of forgotten ambushes still lies where the shock of the action threw it—the rust-red tank with the bomb crater beside it, and the splintered gun overthrown by the same explosion, and, frozen in their last throes, the trucks which perished in front of them just as they first came in to sight round the bend. More often than not the back drop to these pieces contains a single farm house which caught fire during the action and crumbled slowly to ruins, the thatch settling down feather-light on the rubble heap like an eiderdown of bright purple patches, each blade of grass still distinct in the fabric, and a light frost now over all. In the larger villages what remains of the walls of the few stone buildings stand up out of these mauve seas, and on some of them the remains of notices welcoming the United Nations still flap in the wind. But the country village—the grass-thatched settlement of mud huts—is now represented simply by a low, wide mound of violet ashes with a forest of jointed earthenware pipes, the chimneys from the basement, sticking up out of it like some very queer grove of bamboos.

Under the ashes the dead lay all winter, and it was not until their decay in the spring sunshine threatened Korea with epidemics more horrible than high explosive that anything was done about them.

Groups of squatters had patched together hovels of beaten tin and corrugated iron with the surrounding debris and lived some sort of life in the ruins. On one wrecked tank two little girls had made a swing. Any more or less complete building was the billet of some army supply unit. All along the road we heard tales of guerillas and recently ambushed convoys, but though we often saw their handiwork, including some very fresh corpses, they never troubled us.

It was at about four o'clock on the second evening out of Taegu (we stopped one night in a big building in Taejon which still had a roof and was Transport H.Q.) that we ran into an atmosphere shaken by distant artillery fire. The battle was not far away either, for in one village a telegraph pole hit by a flame thrower was still burning. We were looking for a particular unit and our way led off the Main Supply Route and down a track no bigger than an English footpath which wound about among ridges where not even the wreck of a single farmhouse broke the austerity of snow and grey sky, until, climbing a pass, we noticed that the ridge to the left of us was stippled all over with grey patches. They were Chinese corpses, and the first enemy dead I had yet seen. Someone was advancing, then, and advancing, apparently, with great spirit and determination, for the nearest corpses were lying spreadeagled, bent backwards with their feet still dangling in their shallow foxholes—and they had all been bayoneted. Robbins and I padlocked the jeep's gears and brakes together and walked out along what was afterwards known as 'Turks' Ridge.'

As might have been expected, it was the Turks who had dented a great gap in the enemy lines with the bayonet. There were 800 bodies on the ridge, and nearly every one of them had died that way. The bodies were scattered all over the ridge top and the first quarter of its southern slope. Ice-hard in the frost, the Chinese looked very young and rather fine and delicate. They didn't wear the padded khaki winter clothing of the North Koreans, but merely three or four layers of thin cotton cloth: their shoes and boots were all so badly down-at-heel that they might well have marched in the same pairs all the way down from Manchuria. I went through the pockets of one soldier; he was carrying absolutely nothing but an ammunition clip, a small bone seal for signing his name, and one of the 'safe-conduct for prisoners' passes which were being dropped by thousands over the enemy every day urging them to surrender.

At the bottom of the slope, a glitter of tins showed the positions from which the battalion of Turks had sprung up the slope.

It had been about one o'clock in the morning, the Turkish Commander, General Yazici told me, later.

"I passed the word around," he said, "that this was the same unit on top of the ridge which had cut us up so badly at Kunuri,

164

where we were surrounded and fought our way out through miles of ambushes. My men went up the slope as if they were running a race."

That slope was about as much as I could walk up: it must have been 400 yards high and a climb of about one in six.

The Turks were altogether surprising people. They had a Brigade Group in Korea, and from the start set a standard of soldiering which made them a legend. They are supposed to have complained bitterly in one battle that the artillery fire put in to soften the enemy position before their charge had been so heavy that there had not been enough active Chinese left on the hilltop to put up an interesting fight.

General Yazici, when I went to see him at his Brigade H.Q., turned out to be a charming and formidable personality. He lived in a little square tent which stood in a clearing by itself, and you could almost touch the aura of authority which emanated from it. Steps became slower, voices lower, consciences less easy as they approached this shrine of military virtue. The Turkish soldiers lived under an iron discipline; they were smarter in their bearing and their camp was neater than any others I visited in Korea. General Yazici, physically a small man in his fifties, had a remarkably intelligent and expressive face, not the kind of face whose distinction is derived from long habit in a narrow range of noble emotions, but a complicated, mobile, vital face, humorous, wise, comprehending, authoritarian and always and especially formidable. He spoke French well and was delighted to find that he could dispense with the services of the interpreter. What the General liked talking about most was the wretched state of the Korean people. He dismissed my cautious and flattering leads to conversation about the Turks in battle—all he would say in a response to references by name to his better-known actions was: "Yes, yes, that was a hard fight, but consider the terrible state of this country—the children—it is enough to make one weep. What can we do for them? We give them food and they go on down the road to die somewhere else."

The Turks were popular with everybody—and that includes that not very often included element, the South Korean people.

Turkish camp fires always had their rabble of refugee children around them, sharing the soldiers' food.

The General had his Korean servant sent in so that he could show off his Turkish, acquired in three months with the Brigade. It was first-class, the General said, and he kept interrupting the catechism with an explosive "Bon, bon." Then we went outside to see the prisoners, three dreary-looking North Koreans in padded clothes and a Chinese, who had all been so well dusted with DDT powder that they looked like millers. They were smoking Turkish cigarettes, squatting on the ground, and the only sense we could make of them in half an hour with the interpreter was the cackle of obviously unfeigned laughter which they set up when it finally dawned on them that we really were asking the absurd question, "Did you volunteer for the army?"

On Turks' Ridge, then, as the sun began to set and the frost to bite, I first made acquaintance with the desired end-product of all this vast machinery of trucks and aeroplanes and dumps and ships and tanks and factories—the small dead bodies of the enemy.

Robbins and I arrived at Pyongtek, our destination, in the blackness of a moonless night. For the last three miles of our journey the whole countryside was illuminated by an enormous fire, which showed the Korean road police, muffled in their sandbag enclosures, and the outlines of ghostly villages. It turned out to be a bonfire in what might have been called Pyongtek's village green. "What's that for?" I asked the officer who welcomed us into our new billet. "Oh, that's the local labour exchange," he said, and indicated a group of Korean children sitting around it peeling our potatoes.

5

The push up the centre was going well, but it was still in some ways a queer, unsatisfactory kind of war. The early faith of the American troops that the whole thing could somehow be got over by machinery, without much human risk, had faded and there was a growing recognition that fabulous expenditure of material was not, perhaps, a military virtue in its own right.

There had been a certain pious and devotional quality about, for instance, the burning of great parks full of trucks on the road from Pyongyang, all of which could easily have been brought back. It was felt obscurely that expenditure, not saving, won wars.

This feeling was beginning to fade, but the ideal of 'no unnecessary risk to human life' was still carried to very great length. If an advancing platoon were held up by an enemy machine gun, the practice was to telephone back for an aeroplane or the artillery to do something about it. Nevertheless, the army as a whole was waking up. It looked and felt tougher. It was prepared to get out of its vehicles and soldier, if the necessity arose. It had begun to succeed.

Exactly how and why the army was transformed in a few weeks from a mob of dispirited boobs still thinking in terms of a 'press-button war' to a tough and resilient force is still a matter for speculation and debate. I think most of the credit is due to General Ridgway, who had decided there were to be no more 'bug-outs.' Other factors which always crop up in debate on the subject are these:

It is said that the Americans, who do not care for failure, had themselves just reached the pitch of 'getting mad' when General Ridgway arrived.

It is said that the winter had already weeded out those in all the armies to whom soldiering in Korea was intolerable at any price, since a man had only to remove his boots and socks for a few minutes to be a serious frost-bite casualty.

Another factor was the ordinary period of acclimatisation. Those who didn't sicken in the winter were toughened by it.

All these factors had their influence. What happened was that the army quite suddenly began to fight, and in the process integrated itself. By the time the Gloucesters did their star piece of soldiering in late April the United Nations had an integrated force, tough, high-spirited, experienced and, within ordinary limits, internally friendly. That was a great achievement.

CHAPTER XIX

1

TWENTY-NINE Brigade was in action on the central front.
It was the sort of action described in the communiqués as
'steady gains on the central front.' The troops were moving
on foot up and down the cruel hills one by one, combing out
the Chinese and holding each hill until its possible outflankers
were in friendly hands. It was tough, primitive infantry stuff,
greatly eased by an intensive effort of air support.

"It's a tough grind for the old men," said the commander of
the Royal Northumberland Fusiliers, Colonel Kingsley Foster.
"If you want to see what this sort of fighting is like, you had
better come out with us tomorrow. At one place, if all goes well,
we shall have a wonderful view of the whole battle from our
hilltop, and can watch the Gloucesters take that feature," and
he pointed to a mountain massif about two miles away.

2

The Colonel's battalion headquarters was at the far end of a
long, narrow valley with almost precipitous sides, a cul-de-sac
whose end was a steep hill or bank much lower than the sour-
rounding peaks. When we had climbed to the top of this bank
we were in No Man's Land. It was a queer world he led me
into, utterly still and white, the landscape of a children's fairy
story done in sugar icing. The spiral foot tracks which wound
about the hillsides were invisible at five yards distance, for six
inches of fresh snow had moulded them into the landscape.
The wind had ceased to blow, the air was diamond bright and
the ice-skin on the snow glittered and sparkled in the sunshine.
When we spoke our voices were thin and without any resonance

The " A-Frame "   *(Planet News)*

Advance across the Han River   (*Planet News*)

29 Brigade Sector, Imjin River   (*Planet News*)

and seemed to fall away gently into the deep silence of some gully or ravine, thrown away like wastepaper.

Colonel Kingsley Foster was a stout, full-blooded man and I was surprised at the form he showed scrambling along, often hand over hand up a track which described the fancy figure-eights and swooping slopes of a giant switchback at a funfair. He had to wait for me several times and I must have been ten years his junior. In less than half a mile my heart was pounding at bursting point and the muscles at the backs of my knees were knots of pain.

"This is the ticklish bit," said the Colonel, as we merged from a tiny pass between two peaks to find another two of them in front of us. "You see, we haven't occupied that hill at all, and the Chinese may still be on it. They've made no signs of being there, but that's part of their tactics. They may just be lying there and waiting until the whole area has been bypassed and then they'll start playing hell with a mortar or two in the lines of communication. The point is, though, that the other peak beyond this one has to be held by us during the Glouces-ters' assault on the main position and we haven't time to deal with this hill before they go into action: we are just having to assume for the moment that it's not held by the enemy. And I should advise a little caution here, because the next 300 yards of our track is right bang in the Chinese field of fire, supposing they do hold that hill. They may not think it worth while to pot just the two of us, though, even if they're there."

We went pretty fast between the spots of cover on that stretch, but not the faintest movement stirred the remote, aloof landscape around us, and as we turned into safety with a hilltop between us and the unexplored peak we could see X Company, the Fusiliers, beginning to make their assault on the next, a gigantic peak ahead of us.

The soldiers swarmed up the steep cone of the hill in aston-ishing time. They were strung out along the whole side of it which was turned to the sun and we saw three figures flitting very fast from cover further up the slope: they fled round to the dark north side. It was just like putting up hares. Rifle fire sounded in a thin crackle and one of the figures gave a queer leap and came rolling very fast down the steep mountainside. The others, so far as we could see, got away round the back to the main Chinese position which the Gloucesters were to take.

"I thought so," said the Colonel, "they are not going to bother about defending this peak, it's the Gloucesters' hill they're worried about." The Fusiliers flushed four more of the enemy from covered positions as they approached the top of the peak. They killed two of them and wounded another, but the fourth man could be seen running very fast to the safe dark side of the hill, and though a dozen rifles crackled in his wake he seemed to have made a clean get-away. It was a very tough climb to the top of that peak, and when the Colonel and I arrived the company commander had already posted men where they could look out for movement on the further ridge, the Gloucester massif, and the rest were 'brewing up' on the reverse slope. The field telephone was already working, and there was a feeling of pleasure abroad because the hill had been so lightly occupied by the enemy. 'A piece of cake,' in fact.

Except for the great square mountain mass in front of us to the north, separated from us by a valley half a mile wide and 2,000 feet deep, our peak was the highest point in the visible area. We looked down upon a landscape brutal in its endless reiteration of the same threat, the same harsh row of jagged teeth repeated over and over again until the eye lost the last one beneath the curve of the earth. In the valley below us three Centurion tanks, looking about the size of matchboxes, were conspicuously black on the wrinkled tablecloth of the rice paddy terrraces.

One of the Fusiliers in cover on the forward slope of our peak now said urgently, "There they are, sir. Movement about nine o'clock of lone tree. Four or five of 'em." In the silence which followed, while all eyes peered at the one stark little tree opposite us, an aeroplane droned by on its circular beat, vulture-like 2,000 feet above us, and then four or five voices spoke at once. "Yes, there they are. Got 'em, sir. Must be a dozen. Behind that little hump."

"Get 45th Field on 'em," said the Colonel, referring to the artillery, "just give the map reference."

170

A young officer wearing one of the newly arrived British winter hats—a sort of sealskin tea-cosy—spoke sharply into the telephone and then stopped. We waited about twelve seconds. We heard no bang from the guns below and behind us, but a melancholy syllable like a sharp moan or a plucked 'cello string sounded in the air above us. The first shell was on its way. Three seconds later a delicate bush of smoke expanded in the brilliant air near 'Lone Tree' and we heard the crack of the explosion. Then we could all see the enemy—a dozen tiny figures running along the mountain just below the ridge with the bush of smoke expanding in their midst. The officer telephoned again and the shells began to utter their enigmatic monosyllables above us in quick time. Men crawled forward to watch the results.

"Get into cover," said Colonel Foster sharply, "there may be a mortar over there."

We were pressing ourselves forward into the ground before he had finished speaking as an ominous whisper grew against the sobs of the shells.

Fyuff-yuff-yuff-yuff-yuff and CRASH!

A very good shot too. It burst on the forward slope and kicked dirt and snow across us. Then another. Then another.

And now somebody else took a hand in the action. The two Corsairs, wheeling idly like vultures above the Gloucesters' objective, suddenly began a purposeful prowling to and fro across the ridge top, then they hauled off, came racing round the back of our hill in a wide sweep, and then the leading one seemed to gather itself and spring like a panther towards the ridge. It tore through the sky with a noise like tearing oilcloth, and suddenly there was a red path of flame between its nose and the mountain top. Five seconds later we heard the crunch of its guns—a noise of impossible violence and hate. It wheeled out of circuit, and the second one came in to repeat the performance. The mortar fire stopped.

Five minutes later it began again, though, and the Corsair, with the air of someone who has now finally lost all patience, came screaming in again, circled, slowed, tipped a wing neatly over 'Lone Tree' and 'tossed,' as it were, negligently, a long, yellow, banana-shaped object over the knife edge of the ridge. It fell slowly, turning over and over, and where it landed a dark red flame grew and spread outwards in waves until it covered a great area. Black smoke went up. The sound which came to us later was a sort of lax explosion. 'Floomf,' it said.

"That's napalm," said the Colonel to me, "jellied petrol. It reaches a temperature of more than 1,000 degrees Centigrade in a few seconds. Horrible stuff."

And as the flames died into flickering grass fires, the tiny figures of the Gloucesters could be seen swarming up the lower slopes of the mountain and the tank guns began to go 'Whop-Whop' in the paddy fields. The assault had begun. It was a tough action. The slope was so steep that it was a matter of hand-over-hand climbing, and the Chinese were well dug in around the mountain top. They kept a strong fire from rifles and machine guns and tossed their grenades down the slope among the climbing soldiers.

The Gloucesters reached the summit very late in the afternoon.

"All right, then," said Colonel Foster, after a spell at the field telephone, "dig in. All round defence. I've told them to send up the bedding."

As we walked back to battalion H.Q. he said: "Well, that's what it's like. We can take about two of these features in a day if they're only lightly defended. Then we sit on the top and wait for what they all call 'the patter of little feet'—the Chinese night attack, the counter-attack. A good many of these Reservists are men in the middle thirties and it's very exhausting going for them, day after day. It will take us a long time to get back to the Yalu River, if that's where we're going, if we have every one of these hills to climb on the way—and that really is the only way to win this war, by hard, primitive foot slogging."

At the foot of the peak the Fusiliers occupied, a single file of Koreans, bent low under piled A-frames toiled along the track, sweating. They were the Fusiliers' porters and were carrying the bedding and other stores for the night.

"I claim that we are the only unit which has properly adapted itself to Korea," said the Colonel; "we've bought some bullocks and hired Koreans to drive them, and we've engaged these porters; they halve the work. Of course, in a few weeks' time, when spring comes, we shan't have to cart all this bedding about."

He stood by the side of the track beaming at the porters and saying a word to each toiling man as he passed: "Thank you. Thank you very much, Number One. Very good. Thank you."

"When next you go to Tokyo, my boy," the Colonel said to me, "see if you can get me a couple of bottles of claret: I haven't had a really civilised drink for months."

3

All along the front in February and March the United Nations were footslogging slowly forward in remote valleys and gulleys, and on the tops of peaks where probably no man had ever before set foot. The Turks and the French grew famous for their bayonet charges. All day, every day and all night, too, the air forces and the artillery pounded away at the enemy positions, and the villages in which they were billeted. The Eighth Army moved slowly forward through such a scene of desolation as can rarely have been seen before. Korean villages of wattle and mud and grass thatch burn very easily, and a very small bomb can bring a whole flimsy village down about its owners' ears. Acre after acre of the poisonous-looking mauve and violet ashes spread across the face of Korea, and rows of scarred and splintered telegraph poles leaning at odd angles marked the little towns and villages which the enemy had once occupied.

One such town, which I saw within twenty minutes of its capture, sticks in my memory like a nightmare. The shelling had brought down the tops of two telegraph poles and welded them together into a sort of abstract sculptor's 'form' which stood on its two legs fifteen feet high in the middle of the main street at a cross-road. The splintered butts by the roadside were still burning. All around stretched the still smouldering acres of ashes; under the abstract 'work' a corpse, bolt upright by some trick of contraction set up by the napalm which had killed him, sat hideously grinning, and smouldering all over.

His arm had contracted into a caricature of a Communist salute. Just beyond him, to frame the picture, a bridge had collapsed in the most graceful folds and convolutions of metal and concrete into the shape of a twisted fan. It was a day of brilliant, shining calm with the smoke from the ashes going straight up in casual spirals like cigarette smoke. The white peaks stood all around, as grand as statues.

In a clear space ten miles beyond this town a week or so later 29 Brigade H.Q. had established itself. The Siberian wind was back with us, and whistled along the river bed whose bank was the Brigade area. The Red Crosses on the ambulances and medical tents shouted across all that whiteness like bugle calls. They could be seen for miles. The sun shone and there was a mutter of guns in the air.

I was sitting gossiping with Tubby Marshall in his little caravan when the field telephone buzzed. Tubby picked up the receiver, "Yes, Yes Doc. Yes, he's here now. Right, I'll tell him."

"That's the Doctor," he said to me, "and he seems to be in a great rage about something. He says if you'll go along to the Field Hospital, he has something to show you."

I met the doctor striding impatiently over the snow to meet me. He grabbed my arm.

"Look, we must have some publicity about this. Perhaps the Press can make these people wake up to a sense of their responsibilities. Look at this, I want to show you this," shouted the doctor as we came into a clear space in front of the hospital tent.

In front of us a curious figure was standing, a little crouched, legs straggled, arms held out from his sides. He had no eyes, and his whole body, nearly all of which was visible through tatters of burnt rags, was covered with a hard black crust speckled with yellow pus. A Korean woman by his side began to speak, and the interpreter said, "He has to stand, sir, cannot sit or lie."

He had to stand because he was no longer covered with a skin, but with a crust like crackling which broke easily.

"That's napalm," said the doctor, "and I'm not going to argue about the rights and wrongs of using it. Not my job. But somebody's got to start looking after these chaps, that's the twenty-fifth this week at this hospital alone, and in the battalions the doctors have had even more. Now listen. I cannot deal with these people; they are gangrenous and would infect my wounded. I have no transport to evacuate them in, and there's nothing I can do for them on the spot. This man is going to die; but if he could get six months of devoted nursing, he would probably pull through. He'll be blind, of course, and I think this case is probably mentally affected as well, but he could be saved. The arrangements at present, so far as I can find out, are for 'walking wounded' civilians to report to police stations, where they are kindly allowed to sit around until they die. This man is only walking by some miracle. God knows how he got here; he has come six miles from a village up there in the hills."

He took me into an extra tent which he had put up in the area and showed me four more civilian cases—a baby, with the side of its face one great black burn, a girl who had all one leg in the same condition and two men with minor burns.

"With these cases," said the doctor, "I can help. I can give them the right stuff and tell their relations what to do to help them. I've had half a dozen children here with shell-fire wounds, too. Tetanus and gangrene kill most of them."

I thought of the hundreds of villages reduced to ashes which I, personally, had seen and realised the sort of casualty list which must be mounting up along the Korean front.

The burnt man's story was a simple one. As he stood shaking in front of us muttering his answers, the interpreter told us that he was a tram driver from Seoul. He had fled at the Chinese approach, and quartered himself on relations in the remote village far from the fighting. One day the Chinese army came in and billeted itself on the people. Next day the place was napalmed.

"He says he was a long way from where the bomb fell," the interpreter told us, "but some of the burning material in it flew through the air and drenched him from head to foot. He has been living since then with this woman, his cousin, and all yesterday he walked until he came to the Red Cross."

"If only there were some civilian hospital," said the doctor. "What am I to do?"

He did manage, in fact, to arrange to transport the tram driver to Suwon, where some sorely overworked helpers from Civil Assistance Command might be able to do something for him, and it is only fair to state here that Civil Assistance Command had an impossible job which they very nearly succeeded in making into a great success. In less than a fortnight after this incident they had arranged civilian hospitals and a scheme for the evacuation of the wounded. Later, a Civil Assistance Officer was attached to each division of the army.

It was in these weeks of mountain warfare that the United Nations army found its salvation. As its efficiency grew week by week, its internal dissensions began to disappear: 29 Brigade to whom the epithet 'The Old Man's Brigade' had been applied when they first appeared in Korea (and the name was not kindly meant), now wore the title as an honour. 'The Old Men,' the Reservists, preoccupied with their varicose veins and other minor weaknesses of the flesh during the slogging daytime marches, and with problems of money and family matters in the night-time, when they waited for the 'patter of little feet,' had turned out to be tougher than most of the human material dispatched by the nations to Korea. They didn't wear their rows of campaign ribbons for nothing. They knew a good deal, and didn't waste themselves in futile activity or noise. In the crucial moment they could be relied upon to any extent.

4

General Ridgway's plan came off. The enemy withdrew from Seoul to save his flank. Nobody took much notice, and the first patrol into the city consisted almost entirely of correspondents. I went in about three days later with Tubby Marshall. Seoul was silent, empty and cold, a charred ruin. The tramlines sagged within a few feet of the roads in many places and you could easily lose your head if you drove about there in a jeep at night. Bomb and shell holes in the roads increased the driving hazards, and there was a new danger—mines. The Chinese had salted every main artery with enormous mines made in wooden boxes and undetectable by ordinary methods. They were ingenious mines, constructed so as to have the most devastating moral effect, inasmuch as it was quite difficult to be sure of exploding them. Not the first vehicle, but the hundred and first which went over the mine was the more likely to be blown up. Some were so constructed as to be quite safe for forward-moving traffic but deadly for returning vehicles. Tubby Marshall and I took our jeep under the railway bridge four times that day. Next day an unlucky carrier belonging to the Eighth Hussars blew up on the same spot.

The few old people and children left in the city had no very dramatic tale to tell. The main body of the Chinese had camped for the whole of their stay in the northern outskirts of the city. The officers and special detachments who had entered Seoul had behaved well. When they left, they rounded up the entire able-bodied population and took them north with them.

Whether purely by accident, or by some incomprehensible form of discrimination, the Chinese had left some large, warm useful buildings entirely untouched; others they had ransacked. They left the American Embassy in utter chaos, for instance, but the British Embassy presented an almost comical air of unconcern—there were golf clubs in the hall and dust-covers on the furniture: tea on the lawn seemed to be the programme for the afternoon. In the Chosen Hotel, which had been untouched by the fire, the Christmas decorations still hung from the walls and ceilings. HAPPY XMAS, said the notices, and the Christmas trees' tinsel still glittered in the cold, dark hall.

29 Brigade had been switched from the central front to their old position in front of the capital, and now they beat their way slowly up to Uijongbu, a flat ruin, and beyond, until late in March, with their lines of communication strung out along twenty-five miles of barbarous tracks and paths which two or three well-directed bombs could have made impassable, they came to a halt just south of the Imjin River, which was to be the left flank of the United Nations line, and sat across the classic route of entry into Seoul.

5

And then spring came very suddenly. There was suddenly a day when everyone exclaimed at butterflies and the rice paddy

was found to contain not ice but water—and water with a tinge
of green life in it, and a thin black smoke of gnats dancing on
the surface of it. People moved about in shirts and trousers and
the cook sang in the sunshine as he peeled the potatoes. With
the end of winter, half the horror of the war vanished, and for
a few weeks Korea was a lovely land: its ancient poetic name,
'Chosen'—The Land of the Morning Calm—was no longer a
wry joke but something delicately appropriate to the country's
mood. The water-sheets flashed in the sun from the ends of
narrow valleys, where in the distance larch trees bore a barely
visible foliage, transparent clouds of soft green. Great white
cranes glided across the paddy fields with an archaic and dream-
like dignity, and a little later the whole theatre set of hills and
peaks broke out in millions of pink flowers.

And with all this loveliness a new menace arrived. The
unburied dead, the half-empty tins of food, the ordure and
excrement left lying all about the country under the restraining
frost, now shook off their inhibition and blossomed too—into
an appalling smell which hung over the peninsula from end to
end.

And with the sunshine, new notices appeared on the decaying
telegraph poles along the M.S.R. One read TYPHUS in red
letters, another SMALLPOX in black, and they warned the
traveller of infected areas.

Upon me, at any rate, these two notices had as great a shock
of impact as the famous one about mines which appeared at
about the same time. This mine notice had been devised to
keep Death off the Roads: it was an appeal to keep clear of the
mine-sown verges of the tracks. On a blood-red board appeared,
most realistically, a skeleton, and underneath it, in white, the
words, YOU TOO, CAN HAVE A BODY LIKE MINE.

It was with these events that the soldier in Korea was concerned and diverted at the time when, suddenly, all the correspondents grabbed their typewriters and fled to Japan, for the
impossible had happened, the mighty had fallen: General
Douglas MacArthur was recalled to the United States.

We watched him go in the early morning through streets
lined with hundreds of thousands of Japanese citizens gravely

bowing as he passed. We noted once again the astonishing vigour and vitality, the presence and personality which any great actor might have envied, and then he was gone, and a great anticlimax settled on Tokyo. Echoes of the controversy that was shaking America were only dimly and professionally noted in that city, and an unusual tact and delicacy prevailed in the Press Club, where it was assumed by the Americans that the British were glad of the General's departure and probably responsible for it, in part; the British believed their views to be unpopular and were prepared to sympathise with the Americans on the downfall of an idol, or at least to hold their tongues, on a matter which, they felt, was an American domestic quarrel; and neither side said much, because the United Nations had grown up enough to wish to avoid dissension.

The *Saturday Review* sent every correspondent in Tokyo a questionnaire on the subject. While I was filling mine in an American at the next table in the Club broke not only the immediate silence, but the restraint of days, and said to me: "Let's see what you've written."

I handed it over. He read it and gave me a brief smile.

"Pretty much what I've said, and, for your information, I'll bet it's pretty much what all of us have said."

(When the *Saturady Review* published its results he was found to have been correct. The great majority of journalists in the Far East theatre of war had declared that Mr. Truman had been right to dismiss the General.)

And while the controversy screamed on in the States, and Tokyo was full of stories about the new broom General Ridgway would bring to the Dai' Ichi building, and those G.I.s who used to walk abroad in the city with silk notices sewn to the backs of their combat suits proclaiming that they had 'Returned from Hell' disappeared and were seen no more, and fat officers trembled in their boots because of notices addressed to OBESE PERSONNEL, and the Festival of Blossom Time began in Japan, the dreary stalemate across the water continued. Then, early one morning, the *Nisei* girl at the telephone exchange in the Press Club began to chant my name. When I picked up the telephone a very faint voice belonging to a British officer, a friend of mine in Korea, said: "I can't say anything much because this phone is under Security Regulations. It's just this —you ought to try to get here as quick as you can."

I didn't wait for any more. The new Chinese offensive had started, then. I was in a plane in half an hour. I reached 29 Brigade in time for the last act of the glorious battle of the Imjin River.

CHAPTER XX

I

Even to a man flitting through Korea as fast as I was going, it was obvious that the spirit of the times was against any more 'bug-outs.' At Taegu, in the hot sunshine, the jets came tearing off the runway every ten seconds. There was a new spirit abroad. Nobody said, "What are we here for?" Nobody said, what was almost worse, "Hell, we've got 'em licked." A young American air force officer walked across to me while I was waiting on the strip for the jets to give my plane a chance to get away.

"I hear the British are in a big fight up there," he said, " and I hear they've knocked the hell out of the Chinese, in the first round, anyway. D'you know how they're doing?"

"No," I said, "I'm going up to find out."

"I'll be there before you," said the young man, and he pointed towards the jet planes. "I fly one of these, and I'm taking off for the Imjin River sector in fifteen minutes."

At Suwon they had made the big crashed C 54 on the airport perimeter into a Press Centre. THE WORLD'S MOST FAMOUS CORRESPONDENTS PASSED THROUGH THIS DOOR, said a notice above it.

The P.I.O. captain, thank heaven, was at his American best.

"Jeep? Sure. I can get you a jeep in approximately twenty minutes. Sit down while I get you some eggs. D'you need a typewriter? Got enough paper, pencils? Here's a map. That's your best route. No whisky, but I got plenny coffee. Relax. Yes, the battle's all along the front. Very heavy attack. British sector? Yes, they're holding. Some boys of yours called the Gloucesters? Well, they say they got the brunt of it in that sector, but I only got that unofficially. No hard news, and a forty-eight hour strict censorship." He put a great dish of fried eggs and bacon in front of me and rang the telephone.

"Yep. I wanna jeep. No. Now. O.K. Yes, going right up front. It'll be here in about fifteen minutes," he told me. "I can let you have blankets, only send them back when you've done with 'em."

Seoul was full of guns.

They stood in the city streets and around its perimeter. There seemed to be hundreds of them, mostly 105's and 155's. This Chinese spring offensive was going to be the test piece. Early in the afternoon my jeep swung into Brigade H.Q.

2

The 29th Independent Infantry Brigade Group had a front-line strength of about 4,000. Its infantry consisted of the 1st Battalions, the Royal Northumberland Fusiliers, the Royal Ulster Rifles and the Gloucestershire Regiment, and it had also the Belgian battalion under command. The Eighth Royal Irish Hussars supplied most of the armoured strength with their enormous Centurion tanks—fifty-two tonners for which no more difficult country than Korea could ever have been found; there were only occasional patches in the whole peninsula where these tanks could manœuvre, or even turn round with any ease. The 45th Field Regiment, Royal Artillery, equipped with twenty-five-pounders, with an all-round traverse, were the Brigades' own artillery, but as the big battle wore on, and it became apparent that the brunt of the offensive had fallen on the British Brigade, more and more American artillery turned their attention to that sector.

The Brigade had a 16,000-yard front of very broken country to defend, and its orders were to hold the position at all costs. The Commander, Brigadier Brodie, in view of this order, the nature of the terrain, his private assessment that the attack would come in his area and the fact that his unit was so desperately thin on the ground, asked his commanding general for more men. He was told that no more were available.

As usual in the Korean war, intelligence of enemy movements before the battle was poor, and it was not until a few hours before the Chinese offensive was launched that reports came in of any considerable body of enemy moving south. On the afternoon of the 22nd of April, 1950, the Turks captured a Chinese major who said the offensive was due to begin that very night,

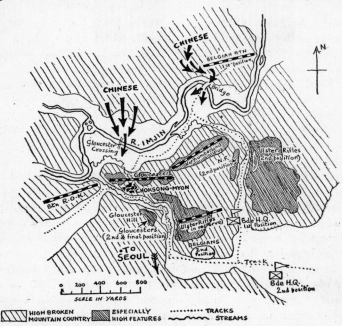

29 Brigade's positions during the battle of the Imjin River

and this information was all the hard fact that anyone had, at any rate on the front's left flank, until the attack began. The Brigade's own patrols across the River Imjin on that day and preceding days had revealed nothing that seemed to indicate an imminent offensive. All previous Chinese offensives had started with strong probing patrols, and there had been none of these. Consequently, the Belgian battalion had been moved across the river and taken up positions north of it on the Brigade's right flank. In the centre, and south of the river, the Brigadier put the Fusiliers: the Gloucesters held the left flank, a piece of exceptionally rugged and broken country opposite the best-known crossing-place on that stretch of the Imjin River. The Royal Ulster Rifles were in reserve.

A fat harvest moon hung above the peaks, shone in the water of the rice paddies and made a golden path across the Imjin River when the battle began. It was a warm, clear night.

The Brigadier walked across to the Press Camp for dinner. He knew by that time that the offensive was coming in that night. It had, in fact, already begun on the Belgian position, but he gave no sign of all this.

"Well, when's this famous offensive going to start?" one correspondent asked him. "Might be tonight," said the Brigadier casually.

"I tell you what, sir, I'll bet you anything you like it doesn't. Go on. Anything you like."

"Oh, I don't think I'll bet on it."

The Belgians were attacked, bypassed and surrounded not very long after six o'clock that evening, and some of the Royal Ulster Rifles were sent off to help them, but the enemy infiltration had been so rapid that they had already crossed the river behind the Belgians, and the Rifles never reached them. The attack began on the Fusiliers at about ten, the Gloucesters were in action not long after midnight, and before dawn the 'sea-wave' was breaking against the whole Brigade. And as the pressure increased it became obvious not only that the Brigade had been singled out to receive the main thrust of the Chinese offensive, but that the whole enemy swing was towards the west and accumulating ever more and more heavily against the Gloucesters' positions.

All the first-hand accounts I have listened to of the Chinese 'sea-wave' tactic tally. The first indication of the attack is the blowing of horns and whistles, and these are believed to be the 'Signals' system the enemy employs, since they are without radio and telephone equipment.

It is said that they choose the period of the full moon so that the shapes of the peaks can guide their units roughly in the right directions, and then the last details of position are settled by signals on whistles and bugles.

The enemy come in massed waves, and the individual soldier

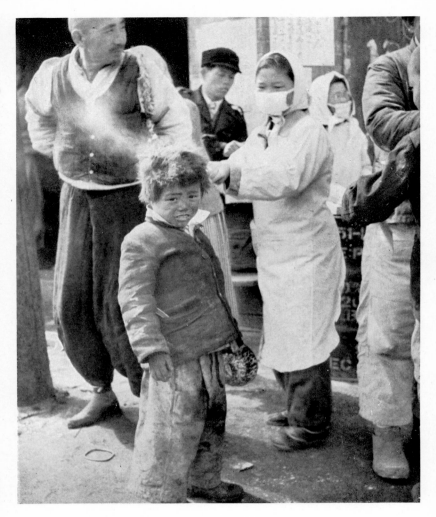

The D.D.T. Squad in Action   (*Planet News*)

The Deserted Village   (*Planet News*)

An Interrogation   (*Planet News*)

seems utterly oblivious of danger. If a shell kills half the men in a marching platoon, the rest march on, unconcerned. At night, only a part of the enemy strength launched against any position is expected to fight there, the duty of the rest is to infiltrate forward and to move on so as to surround and isolate the position as quickly as possible: and this is the manœuvre known in 29 Brigade as 'the patter of little feet.'

The 1st ROKS were on the Gloucesters' left flank, and they were driven back a mile or two pretty early in the battle, so the Chinese were able to move in behind the Gloucesters as early as nine o'clock next morning, St. George's Day. (The Fusiliers and some of the Artillery were wearing their roses during the battle.) By noon, the Gloucesters were not only surrounded, but their B echelon was swamped too, and a great stretch of road almost as far south as Brigade Headquarters was in the hands of the enemy.

What happened on the night of the 23rd/24th is still not quite clear in detail. Signals' telephone wires had all been shot to pieces and wireless communication was bad. Some time during the night the Gloucesters shifted the whole battalion to the top of a high, steep, L-shaped feature 2,000 yards south and west of their old position, dug themselves in, and there they stayed until the battle ended, more than thirty hours later.

The Belgians, meanwhile, had made a miraculous escape from their position, moving out eastwards. They attributed their success in this feat to a mixture of luck and first-class co-operation by the American air force, which always happened to bomb the right hill at the right split second of time. The Belgians moved round to the east of Brigade Headquarters and were almost immediately surrounded again by the force which had moved through the Gloucester B echelon. The Belgians had managed their move so well that they still had almost all their vehicles with them, and there, for the rest of the battle, they stayed, fighting at night under the weird sulphur-yellow light of sodium flares.

At dawn on the 24th some American transport planes which flew over the Gloucester hill to try an airdrop of supplies to them were waved away: the Gloucesters were so hard pressed then that they could not afford to lift the artillery barrage around them long enough to let the planes dive. They had had no food since the second day of the battle, and now they were short of water and of ammunition, using it only when the enemy were so close as to make a 'miss' impossible. They had still twenty-four hours of this kind of fighting to go through. The 'sea-waves' continued to roll up the hill towards them, and all that day the Gloucesters pushed them back. All that day, too, they called down the wrath of the air force and the artillery on the Chinese 'forming-up places' which they could see all around them from their high perch. Their first task was to destroy the enemy, and this they never stopped doing for a moment.

Three attempts to get through to the Gloucesters were made on that day.

A force of Filipino tanks and infantrymen with some of the Eighth Hussars' tanks cruised up seven miles of the Gloucester B echelon road, ambushed nearly all the way in the deep gully, until, when they were within 1,100 yards of Gloucester Hill, the leading tank blew up and the column had to reverse all the way back through the ambush again. Two later attempts by tank columns also failed.

At dawn on the 25th the Gloucesters' position was desperate. Helicopters had not been able to take off the wounded because of the close shell-fire, and also because the steep hill could afford no landing ground for them. The Gloucesters had about 100 stretcher cases on the hill with them. They had had no sleep, no food and no water for more than two days, their ammunition was very low, their hill was a tiny island in a sea of Chinese. Just before dawn, when the Chinese bugle calls and whistles promised a fresh assault, the battalion commander, Lieutenant-Colonel J. P. Carne, ordered the drum-major to blow the 'long reveille.' The battered remains of the Gloucesters, Reservists, with their grousing and their pay problems and their families in Civvy Street, raised a cheer at the bugle call which rang raggedly across the hilltop. At this time one of the companies, whose normal strength was 150 men, had been reduced to fifteen.

Shortly after dawn Brigade told the Gloucesters that they had permission to break out. The enemy was so close then that aeroplanes were machine-gunning them within thirty or forty yards of Gloucester Hill.

It was an hour or two later that the Brigadier sent them the last message they were ever to receive on their rapidly fading wireless set. He said: "Nobody but the Gloucesters could have done it."

What Colonel Carne told the company commanders when he assembled them in a gully on the hillside has been variously reported. The upshot of the conference was that the company commanders were to break out with what was left of their companies, separately. The Colonel and the Sergeant-Major decided to stay behind with the wounded.

Part of what was left of one of these companies came through. Captain 'Mike' Harvey, temporary commander of Dog Coy., is an officer with an unusual personality. His enthusiasm is for judo and he neither smokes nor drinks. He had read somewhere that the Chindits, when they were encircled in Burma, used to make for the direction the enemy came from and then break out sideways behind their main mass.

"Anything was as good as anything else to try in those circumstances," he said.

He watched the other three companies go, and then assembled what was left of his own—altogether rather more than 100 officers and men.

They went out rather fast, but not running, and for three miles met no Chinese at all. It was not until they began the south-bound leg of the journey home that, in a narrow valley, they ran between a terrible fire from both flanks. A Mosquito had spotted them, however, and gave them some confidence as it flew above them guiding them in. And now it wirelessed for fighter planes.

After crawling for miles in a ditch full of sharp stones under whatever extra cover the fighters could provide by keeping the enemy's heads down—and that was not much—they emerged within range of the machine guns of some American tanks. It was a horrible moment for them when the Americans, who were their only hope, mistook them for enemy troops and fired on them. The Mosquito made a great fuss, diving on the tanks and waggling its wings until the Americans realised their mistake. Then they convoyed them in. Dog. Coy. had not been able to stop for any of its wounded, and forty of them were all that returned safely. They were all of the Gloucesters who returned that day, though three more drifted in later.

Meanwhile, on the right flank the Fusiliers and the Rifles were surrounded, and the Belgians on the left of Brigade H.Q. had also to be convoyed through masses of enemy. Ever since the 24th, machine-guns had been rattling even as far south as the Brigade H.Q. perimeter.

The Centurions divided their forces. Eight of them brought out the Fusiliers' and Rifles' wounded through what that tank force's commander described as "one long bloody ambush." The rest of the Fusiliers and the Rifles, with their walking wounded, escaped eastwards.

The other force, convoying the Belgians, arrived at the point where the two roads from the north converged towards Brigade H.Q., just in time to see a whole hillside full of Chinese stampeding down the slope to cut off the exhausted Fusiliers and Riflemen, who had arrived after great hardship at that point. The tank force commander was able to bring his tank between the Chinese and the British and stall off the enemy by backing it 100 yards at a time down the road as he faced them, until the danger of a last encirclement was over.

That was the end of the Battle of the Imjin. The Brigade sustained more than 1,000 casualties. There are no official estimates of the Chinese casualties, but it is known that three Chinese divisions were flung against the Brigade during those three days, and that the Chinese army time-table was so badly disorganised as a result of these divisions' reception by the British that the idea of taking Seoul as a May Day present for the Kremlin had to be abandoned. Not long afterwards the whole Communist push in the Seoul sector was called off.

It was not long before it became apparent that the Chinese spring offensive had altogether failed, that the whole experiment had failed. The Communists had proved for themselves, once and for all, that a modern army of moderate size, determined and well-equipped, could withstand the assault of great masses of ill-equipped, old-fashioned infantry, no matter how courageous or fanatical they might be. The easy conquest of the civilised world by millions of expendable Asians had turned out to be a futile dream.

CHAPTER XXI

I

In a remote valley less than two miles from the scene of that battle, a tiny grass-thatched cottage clung to a slope above a single strip of field and about twenty yards of rice paddy. A great black patch on the hillside within a yard or two of the farm showed how nearly a napalm drop had missed it.

The farmer, an old man, dressed in stiff white country clothes, with the black horse-hair top hat of seniority, smoked his three feet of bamboo pipe with the brass bowl and gazed placidly at his holding.

His wife, astonishingly wrinkled and bowed, fetched and carried across the field the heaps of straw and fertiliser. She toiled in the sun indefatigably. The old man watched and smoked.

Presently, a heavy tank ground round the corner of the track, and in passing across the edge of the paddy field sluiced a great wave of mud and water over the shining white clothes of the landlord. He continued to smoke. The next time his sweating old wife toiled up with her load to his end of the field he hailed her quietly, took off his outer coat and handed it to her. There and then, she dropped her load of muck, went down to the stream and sat bashing her husband's coat against the stones to clean it. Then she spread it out in the sun and returned to her job of muck-hauling, bent to the straps of her shoulder basket like a draught animal. She had not wasted a moment.

The old man smoked placidly.

My companion, a Korean Catholic priest, whose tiny chapel in Korean style sat higher up on the hill and was miraculously untouched in the ruin of the whole province, said to me:

"That is the real Korea, and it is not a good thing. It is easy to be sentimental about us now that we are suffering. Do you know that if you held a plebiscite in South Korea the Communist vote would be more than seventy-five per cent? We are sick of war and ruin. We are used to masters. Your armies have not behaved well to the people and we dislike you all cordially. It is impossible to keep these great theories of freedom in front of the eyes of simple people. They are afraid of the bombs and the burning and the raping behind the battle line. The Chinese understand us much better, I'm afraid. Your cause is good, but you have lost our good will, and though you all appear to despise us, that is a big thing to lose. In this country, manners count for everything."

That was the last scene I ever saw in the Land of the Morning Calm: the old man and his beast of burden wife, the cranes gliding, ancient and beautiful in the diamond air, the priest commenting acidly.

I was not altogether sorry to go.

2

I was going home. The aeroplane was leaving Tokyo airport for London at seven o'clock next morning.

It had been a good evening, saying goodbye to all my friends. The *tempura* at the *Ten Mo* had been superb, and the friends who helped me eat it, warm and amusing. Mr. Osaka had been moved apparently almost to tears by my imminent departure, and presented me with a special *sake* bottle which I'd always coveted. Even the bank manager protested that he meant well by me. Tokyo was in fine form and had produced a typical incident of the Occupation that week, the story of which, in many versions, was going the rounds.

A certain general in Tokyo was renowned for the extravagance of his rages. When he was in a passion, which was frequently, his eyes 'bugged-out like a tromped-on toad's' and a knot of veins in his forehead wriggled like snakes and he uttered a hissing noise. Nobody, for years, had dared even to look at him in that condition. But the customers of a small bar off the Ginza had been gladdened two days before my arrival, not only to see the General mopping and mowing in his mania, which was a common sight, but to applaud the slight figure of an

American correspondent which was dancing in front of him and shouting: "All right! Have a fit! Have two! Drop dead! Good story!"

I knew and liked this correspondent, and the incident pleased me so much that I was on my way to the Press Club to hear from his own lips what would certainly be a grossly exaggerated, if not an entirely fictitious, account of the event, but which would certainly be worth hearing.

I opened the swing doors. The place was full. At the table nearest the door sat an Australian soldier whom I had met once with his unit at the front. A long, hatchet-faced, thin-lipped Aussie with a crime sheet as long as your arm. He must have been on leave. He sat there in his Australian hat, a cigarette in the corner of his mouth and a great stoup of beer on the table in front of him. His eyes were smouldering ominously. What could he be doing in the Press Club? He had no right in there at all.

I was about to go over and slap him on the back and offer him, as an old acquaintance, the protection of my membership, when I saw that I had been forestalled. One of the Committee was loping towards him, policeman-like. He put his hands on the Aussie's table top and enunciated in a twang like a banjo: "Are you a member of this club, Young Man? '

The Aussie gave him a level look. "Yew can stick yer nose in a dead bear's bum," he said, and returned to his drinking.

A happy evening. Five minutes later I was listening enthralled to two dramas at once. In my left ear, the riot around the Aussie's table reverberated like a thunder storm; in my right, the correspondent, with the glittering eye of the joyful liar, bellowed his highly diverting account of conversation with the General.

"'Special mission? Don't gimme that. What's your racket?" I said. "Jeeze, I thought he was going to die on me."

The correspondent saw me off at the airport next morning.

"I believe in this United Nations stuff," he said, "but I think it only really comes off among guys who get around a lot and know people. But Jeez, look at the guys who get around! They're crazy! Look at you. Look at me. What do we do it for?

Why don't we stay home and take care of ourselves? What've you got out of going to Korea?"

In the luxurious seat of the airliner, climbing down into London through 30,000 feet of fog two days later, I wondered about this. What had I got out of it? An extraordinary explosive belly-ache for one thing which attacked when I least expected it and left me shaking. The loss of three stones in weight. A heightened blood-pressure. On the other hand, I had met new kinds of people, I had done four stories which I thought were good. The office seemed pleased. But I'd been frightened nearly all the time I was in Korea, horrified very often, uncomfortable always. What was the point? Why do these things?

I shelved the problem. As I sank through the feather bed of fog over London I only knew that the assignment had satisfied some complex craving which in two or three months would be clamouring for satisfaction again.

Not just yet though. I was glad it was over.